Passage to the North

A traveler's companion to the historic sites and frontier legends along the Alaska Highway

William R. Hunt

STACKPOLE
BOOKS

Published by
STACKPOLE BOOKS
Cameron and Kelker Streets
P.O. Box 1831
Harrisburg, PA 17105

Printed in the United States of America

Cover design by Caroline Miller

Cover photo by Alissa Crandall/Alaska Stock Images

First Edition

10 9 8 7 6 5 4 3 2 1

To Alex,
my companion on the highway and in Alaska

Library of Congress Cataloging-in-Publication Data

Hunt, William R.
    Passage to the North : a traveler's companion to the historical
sites and frontier legends along the Alaska Highway / William R.
Hunt. – 1st ed.
        p.   cm.
    Includes bibliographical references (p.173) and index.
    ISBN 0-8117-2409-3
    1. Alaska – Description and travel – 1981- 2. Alaska Highway.
3. Historic sites – Alaska Highway Region. 4. Alaska – History,
Local. 5. Legends – Alaska Highway Region. 6. Hunt, William R. –
Journeys – Alaska. I. Title.
F910.5.H86   1991
917.98 – dc20   91-26856
                                                                  CIP

Contents

Preface

All I had to say to friends and new acquaintances was "I'm working on a history of the Alaska Highway." At once their faces lit up as thoughts of voyages past flooded their memories. Folks still get excited about the highway, as they have always done, and are keen to top any story you offer with one of their own.

From its muddy beginnings as a wartime project, the highway has been known for its pitfalls—perilous bogs, shifting gravel, permafrost collapses, icy stream runoffs, road repair delays, animal casualties, car breakdowns, flat tires, and menace of winter. In this book, intended to be a companion to travelers on the highway, I want to do justice to such experiences but also to set the history in a larger framework.

In 1992 we celebrate the fiftieth birthday of the road laid down by the hardworking U.S. Army engineers—an occasion well worth commemorating. But they were not the first to pass through that land. The country through which the road was driven had been long inhabited by Indians. In fact, the eastern side of the Rocky Mountains was the path of those first Americans who crossed over the Bering Land Bridge 10,000 years ago, then eventually continued their migration south to populate the Americas.

White fur-traders and explorers started coming into the North in the eighteenth century. Later, homesteaders, missionaries, teachers, miners, and others settled in the region and made it their own. I can only touch briefly on pioneer endeavors in British Columbia, the Yukon

Territory, and Alaska, even though these episodes are major events for regions bordering the highway.

Everyone has his own "passage to the North," and I offer my history without claiming it to be definitive or even comprehensive. Don't think I am being modest—just look at the map again, note the extent of that 1,520-mile ribbon, and consider the necessity of a selective approach.

If you are going to Alaska with the intent to remain, you have a particular sense of adventure. Today we cannot be pioneers, but we can gain some appreciation of them on our voyage. The Alaska Highway route is one of the great North American western trails that offered opportunity to people willing to take a chance in new country beyond. In their westering, Americans poured over the Cumberland Road, the Ohio River, the Oregon and California trails, and other routes. Some early users of the corridor to the northwest that eventually became the Alaska Highway also sought a new country. Their numbers were not great, but many were motivated by a distant Promised Land.

Today the Alaska Highway retains its mystique. It is still the way to a new life or to the wilderness for many travelers. If you sense something special, a kind of exhilarating freedom, it is no surprise.

Acknowledgments

I cannot begin to recall the sources of all the stories about the Alaska Highway I have heard in my lifetime. But I can thank the folks who have helped since I began working on this book: Norm and Beth Drayton, Claus Naske, Bruce Merrill, Sande Faulkner, Irmgard Hunt, Robert Spude, Terrence Cole, and the many others along the highway who shared their impressions and told their best stories to me. They also include Terri Hedrick, Paul Whittaker, Hank Vander Giessen, Robert A. Kaye, Eddie Oswald, and Charles Strobridge. My thanks to Wendy Davis, who did the maps. I am especially grateful for the interest and encouragement shown me by Sally Atwater, my editor.

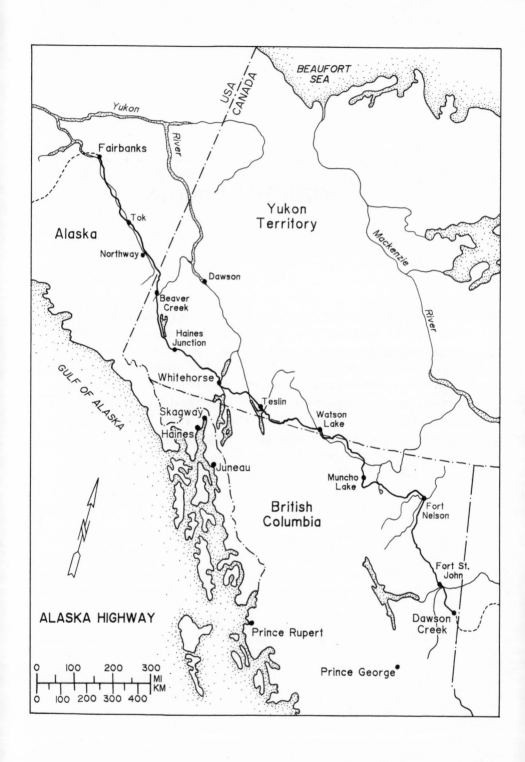

Places and Miles
from Dawson Creek

524.4   Fireside
585.3   Hyland River Bridge
598.7   Lower Post
605.1   B.C.–Yukon Border
612.9   Watson Lake
612.9   Campbell Highway Junction

WATSON LAKE TO WHITEHORSE
626.2   Cassiar Highway Junction
776   Nitsutlin Bay
776.3   Teslin
808.6   Teslin River Bridge
808.9   Johnson's Crossing
836.8   Jake's Corner
        Atlin Road Junction
852.7   Marsh Lake
874.4   Klondike Highway Junction
884   Whitehorse

WHITEHORSE TO THE ALASKA BORDER
943.5   Champagne
985   Haines Junction
1,000.1   Bear Creek Summit
1,029.1   Soldier's Summit
1,051.5   Destruction Bay
1,061.5   Burwash Landing
1,135.6   White River Bridge
1,168.5   Beaver Creek
1,189.5   Alaska-Yukon Border

ALASKA
1,221.8   Port Alcan
1,264   Northway Junction
1,284.2   Tetlin National Wildlife Refuge
1,301.7   Tetlin Junction

The Crooked Road

Big road coming
Don't you hear that sound
Bulldozers smashing
Through rock and ground.
— *The Big Road*

With the advent of World War II and the German invasion of Denmark and Norway in the spring of 1940, American military strategists and congressmen realized that northern Scandinavia was not far from Alaska. Long-distance bombers flying over the Pole could perhaps reach American targets. This dawning of geographic awareness swiftly brought forth money for northern construction projects. Congress allotted almost $40 million for defense installations in Alaska.

Even with huge construction projects under way, including major air bases for Anchorage and Fairbanks, war in the North seemed a distant threat until the Japanese attacked Pearl Harbor on December 7, 1941. The United States responded by declaring war, and at the end of January 1942 A. A. Berle, Jr., the assistant secretary of state, took up the question of a highway to Alaska. As the project had been under consideration for some time, the Canadian and U.S. governments did not take long to come to an agreement.

Controversy over the Route
Planners chose a highway route linking the airfields then under construction in Canada. Canada had developed the idea of an air route in 1935. The Northwest staging route from Edmonton to Alaska was

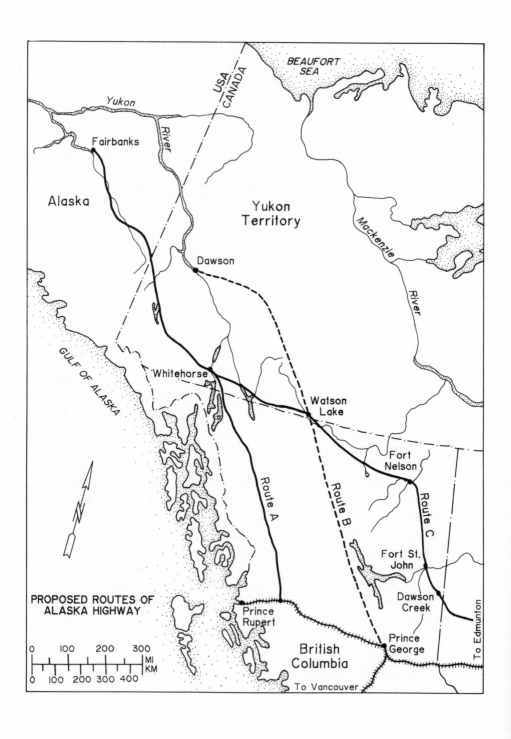

BEAUFORT
SEA

Yukon
River

Fairbanks

USA
CANADA

Alaska

Yukon
Territory

Mackenzie
River

Dawson

GULF OF ALASKA

Whitehorse

Watson
Lake

Fort
Nelson

Route A

Route B

Route C

Fort St.
John

Dawson
Creek

PROPOSED ROUTES OF
ALASKA HIGHWAY

Prince
Rupert

British
Columbia

Prince
George

To Edmunton

0   100   200   300
                    MI
                    KM
0 100 200 300 400

To Vancouver

designed to form part of a great-circle air route to the Orient and avoid the uncertain flying weather of coastal regions. Airfield sites were selected at Grand Prairie, Fort St. John, Fort Nelson, Watson Lake, and Whitehorse. When the war started in 1939, Canadian survey parties were busy laying out the several air bases. The fields were later used to ferry aircraft to the Soviet Union.

As a military decision, the route chosen made sense, but it angered Alaskans and merchants of West Coast cities. Among the most vociferous critics were polar explorer Vilhjalmur Stefansson and Alaskan engineer Donald MacDonald. Stefansson had long advocated a freighting route from the middle of North America toward where northwestern America almost touches northeastern Asia. He envisioned an approximation of the great-circle route following some of those used by the Hudson's Bay Company traders. Travelers would go northwest from Edmonton along the Mackenzie River system to Norman Wells, and from there to the Yukon, Fairbanks, and the Bering Strait.

MacDonald, justly called the father of the Alaska Highway, also objected. When World War II discussions of the highway started, the sixty-two-year-old engineer had been thinking and writing about the road for fourteen years. With his long experience in northern construction, no one could have been more ready and able to advise the U.S. Army Corps of Engineers on the road project.

In 1936 President Franklin Roosevelt had appointed MacDonald and others to the Alaska Highway Commission, established to study the highway's feasibility. Canada, too, formed a commission, and at joint conferences the commissions agreed that the most feasible route would be one nearest the coast, usually called Route A. Route A presented fewer construction difficulties than the two other recommended routes to the east and would effectively tie in with the Alaska cities of the southeastern panhandle. The route would start from Prince George in central British Columbia, keeping east of the coastal range to follow a northwesterly line to Atlin and Whitehorse, then going from Whitehorse to Fairbanks. The Canadian national railroad served Prince George, and the terminus was readily accessible from Vancouver, B.C., and Seattle.

Route B, which followed the Rocky Mountain trench, did not have many boosters. Stefansson's favorite, known as route D, was not taken seriously by anyone. He argued for geographic logic and the availability of petroleum to service the route from the oil field at Norman Wells but got even less support than MacDonald.

The army planners chose route C from Dawson Creek to Whitehorse. MacDonald was outraged by the choice and tried frantically to get a reversal of the decision. He appeared before a congressional committee, wrote a steady stream of letters and magazine and newspaper articles, and tried to focus all the political pressure possible to his cause. But the engineer did not succeed in changing the decision and gained no comfort from following the progress of construction, noting that the terrain problems were as bad as his surveys had shown.

Both MacDonald and Stefansson blamed railroad and Edmonton commercial interests for defeating the logic of the routes they had proposed. Route C backers argued that the Japanese might be able to disrupt road traffic by air attacks if the passage lay too close to the coast, but MacDonald rejected the notion of such Japanese tactics as fantastic. He quoted General Billy Mitchell's statement of 1933 that a supply highway to Alaska should be as near the coast as possible so that the air bases near it could be used to attack an invading enemy fleet.

There is no evidence that commercial pressures affected the U.S. Army's decision to go with Route C. Planners considered the route the best one despite stretches of muskeg—a kind of bog—and mountainous terrain. They were influenced by the construction that was going on for air bases at Fort Nelson and Watson Lake; they saw the value of supporting these bases and also of using their facilities during the road construction.

MacDonald and other Alaskans could not get over the effect of the road decision on the territory's development. Southeastern Alaska is still cut off from road approaches, and the construction of a wartime highway would have been a great boon. Both MacDonald and Stefansson continued to advocate an extension of the highway to the Bering Strait, but in that, too, they were disappointed.

A Certain Wariness
Although the construction scheme offered Canada a number of long-term benefits, including American help with the expensive project, the country showed some resistance to it in the years before the war.

The two nations had a long history of peaceful relations, but Canadians had observed American interference with its neighbors in Latin America on occasion. It was conceivable that a United States presence during construction might become permanent. In some eyes the potential loss of autonomy offset any gains in economic development or benefits to national defense.

P. D. Pattullo, the prewar premier of British Columbia, did not share these apprehensions about American intentions. He tried hard to get the central government's support for a highway, but the costs frightened Ottawa as much as potential Yankee aggression.

Similarly, the U.S. military did not favor the road when it was first proposed. In 1940 planners concluded that the defensive value of a road to Alaska was "negligible" and recommended against construction. The prewar American military planners emphasized the establishment of sea defense routes, and a land defense scheme based on a highway did not interest them.

After Pearl Harbor President Franklin Roosevelt asked the military to consider the Alaska highway plan again. The military planners refused to give the project a high priority but conceded that it would have value and recommended it. Some consideration was given to the postwar advantages of such a highway and the likelihood that Canada would be more favorably disposed to the construction as a war project than as a peacetime one—which was certainly true.

Early on it was understood that the United States would foot the bill for construction and would turn the highway over to Canada after the war. Canada agreed to the construction not because its military considered the road valuable for defense or because of a farsighted view of its potential for economic development, but for political reasons—to avoid offending the United States.

Before the war was over, Canadian officials lost their fear that the highway might represent an American encroachment on territorial sovereignty. The Americans' offer to turn the highway over in 1944 was rejected. Canadian officials reminded the Americans that they had agreed to maintain the highway until the war was over. Canada did not want to carry maintenance costs before it was required to do so.

With the war's end some Canadians were unhappy because the highway was not the first-class project that they believed the Americans had promised them. These critics argued that Canada had never wanted the road in the first place, that the builders did not provide residents with a quality road that would foster economic development, and that it now would require huge expenditures for improvement and maintenance. Concern for intrusion upon Canadian sovereignty gave way to concern for costs. Prime Minister W. H. McKenzie King reminded the critics that buying back the permanent installations built along the highway were investments in sovereignty even if paying $123,500,000 was painful.

You can sometimes still sense the ambivalence of some Canadians about the highway, a project that was thrust upon them. Ottawa's record for fostering northern development was not distinguished until recent years, when arctic petroleum resources encouraged interest, and any highway it might have endorsed would likely have had a different route. But Canadians have generally stopped complaining about the U.S. contribution to northern development. Most can recognize what an enormous benefit the Alaska Highway has been to the country.

Another Canadian complaint concerned the Americans' abandonment of equipment and supplies. Reports differ on whether the American or the Canadian soldiers were responsible for burning some goods, but it was Canada's decision to prohibit the sale of used equipment. The government feared that its manufacturers would be hurt if Canadian buyers were allowed to buy the American equipment, which they were eager to do at bargain prices. The American army had to move everything out of the country at great expense or destroy it. Equipment in good working condition was shipped out. Broken and worn items were destroyed. Those Canadians who were not aware of their government's refusal to permit them bargain purchases viewed the destruction as another example of American wastefulness.

Why Was It Crooked?

But now we are at Dawson Creek, Milepost 0, contemplating a road built in a hurry fifty years ago. Construction projects of the magnitude of this one are in a historic class: Hoover Dam, Panama Canal, transcontinental railroads. Engineering and construction projects may be a matter of mathematics, surveys, logistics, and hard work, but the remarkable ones have a romance about them.

And with romance there are often myths. An anonymous poet once complained,

The Alaska Highway
winding in and
winding out
fills my mind
with serious doubt
as to whether
'the lout'
who planned this route
was going to hell
or coming out.

The once tortuously twisting route of the Alcan Highway (its familiar name until replaced in recent years by Alaska Highway) aroused deep passions among travelers in its early decades. Critics imagined that either incompetence or military strategy had determined the route, neglecting the more obvious possibility that the builders simply followed the path of least resistance. While the poet quoted above echoed a common theory, it ran a distant second to the bizarre notion that engineers had deliberately twisted the route to confuse Japanese bombers or strafers. I have heard this view expressed a number of times by hitchhikers, fishermen, plumbers, housewives, soldiers, runaways, and, amazingly enough, by a communication technician who worked along the highway for twenty-five years.

When folks are reminded that army engineers built more than 1,000 miles of the pioneer road in eight months, they understand its devious course better. A good part of its southern section was through muskeg country; to the north builders ran into permafrost. There were hills and mountain grades to be circumvented. Builders dodged and turned whenever it was feasible.

Construction Start

Getting the job done under wartime pressure was a wonderful feat. Even as the army engineers labored on the pioneer road the work forces of the U.S. Public Works Administration were hard at work improving it. After the war, as the Canadians took over and continued to improve the route, the highway came into its own as the much-needed passage to the North and to Alaska.

The first construction forces reached Dawson Creek in March 1942, arriving by rail from Edmonton, thus following the route used by

Klondike stampeders a half-century earlier. Thousands of soldiers disembarked, with tons of equipment. Other contingents of army engineers and equipment were sent by ship to Skagway, then over the White Pass & Yukon Railway (which the army leased for the construction period) to Whitehorse.

Folks at Dawson Creek were caught up in the excitement of highway construction, and their quiet town changed rapidly as the troops poured in. The scattered residents near the highway route to the north were amazed at the size of the construction forces but generally pleased to see a project that would reduce their isolation and high costs of transportation. Sometimes we hear that the highway outraged Alaskans and forced unfavorable changes in their lives. But there is ample evidence that Alaskans, like northern Canadians, overwhelmingly welcomed the highway.

The Work Forces

The construction forces initially included the 18th, 35th, 340th, and 341st engineering regiments. Later the army added the black 93rd, 95th, and 97th regiments. At the peak of construction the work force comprised 394 officers and 10,765 enlisted men. It was a huge force for a huge job.

The 35th regiment used an existing dirt and gravel road, recently completed by the provincial government between Dawson Creek and Fort St. John, to set up their base at Fort St. John. Between Fort St. John and Fort Nelson the dominion government maintained a winter trail that closed down by April 1 with the spring thaw. Progress in hauling provisions and equipment would have been easier had the 35th been able to start a few weeks earlier. As it was, the trail was already breaking up as the regiment made its first excursions in April.

Bridging the great Peace River at Taylor was the first major undertaking. The river, some 1,800 feet wide at this point, was still frozen as the troops got across. They could not wait for the breakup and ferry service, so they planked the river and spread sawdust over the spongy surface of the ice to retard thawing until they could get their heavy equipment across.

Pushing on to Fort Nelson, the engineers found no easy passage. Muskeg, a marsh formed by thick layers of decaying vegetation, is widespread in the North. During the spring the muskeg froze at night, then partially thawed each day, making movement difficult.

The weather was cold and often windy. The men on foot and on Caterpillar tractors tearing their way through the brush worked hard and maintained a steady pace. Temperatures ranged from fifty degrees above zero to thirty-five below, yet in less than one month, workers got their equipment to Fort Nelson, some 300 miles.

It was important to get the southern section of the road out of Dawson Creek built as soon as possible to expedite shipment of men and materials to the north, where the 35th was at work. The army put two regiments on the segment between Fort St. John and Fort Nelson after the thaw. The 341st got to work first and suffered a major accident in mid-May. Eleven men were drowned when a jerry-built raft sunk in Charlie Lake just west of Fort St. John.

Despite this accident, the 341st carried on. On August 26 the men met soldiers from the 35th who were building a bridge over the Muskwa River near Fort Nelson. Before fall the 341st and the 95th graded, ditched, and built culverts to make a passable road for military traffic from Fort St. John, over Pink Mountain and Trutch, and thence down the Prophet River Valley into Fort Nelson.

Troops were distributed everywhere along the line working west and east in the summer of 1942. It was generally agreed that the 188th and 97th Engineer Regiments working from Whitehorse north to Tok, Alaska, had the toughest country. Not only was permafrost more common there, but the glacial rivers, including the Duke (1,700 feet), the Donjek (1,200 feet), and the White (600 feet), offered the most difficult bridging problems. Crossing the low, boggy country north of the mountains tried the men and their machines. Existing maps were not much help to surveyors, who had to search hard to find the best possible route. Local men who knew the country gladly hired on as guides.

Permafrost

Permafrost, the name given to permanently frozen soil, is common to parts of the northern Yukon and Alaska. Its menace to buildings and roads is obvious if you consider the importance of subsurface stability. Frozen ground is a good support—but only if it stays frozen.

Permafrost is much better understood by engineers and builders today than it was in 1942. Judging from the report of engineer John McGillivray of the Public Roads Administraton, who used packhorses over the route from Jarvis Creek, east of Lake Kluane, to Northway,

Alaska, engineers believed that stripping the ground cover would allow builders to lay their road with ease. "Over practically the entire section of the route reconnoiters," McGillivray said, "swampy terrain is much in evidence, but on detailed investigation, suitable material for road construction was found beneath the matted growth of moss and grass. The mat ranged in depth from six inches to three feet and averaged about one foot in depth." Nothing to it, McGillivray believed. "With adequate drainage and the removal of the muskeg coverage, very good results, I believe, can be obtained."

Although miners and others in the North had been working with permafrost conditions for many years, standard precautions for building on it had not evolved. The army engineers had been trained in temperate climes and did not immediately discover that you cannot build on permafrost with lasting results by removing its insulating mat cover. As the permafrost thawed they attemped to remedy the situation by building countless miles of ditches to drain off the water. Draining, however, was not effective: The water standing in ditches flowed under the road, thawing the permafrost below. The cycle had no end, as the permafrost could be hundreds of feet in depth. In time, too late to prevent rebuilding and rerouting much of the road, engineers learned that they must preserve the mat as well as the ice beneath it in order to support the road.

Progress

Each of the seven regiments was provided with twenty D8 Cats, twenty-four D4 and R4 tractors, fifty to ninety dump trucks, two half-yard gas-powered shovels, six tractor-drawn graders, a truck crane, a portable sawmill, two pile drivers, and numerous Jeeps, cargo trucks, pickups, and carryalls.

Building procedure did not differ from that used on any road job. Parties located the route; Cats made a trail, which was gradually widened; crews felled trees, built culverts and bridges, rough graded, and laid timber for corduroy roads over marshy sections. Meanwhile, other crews followed behind to improve grades and spread surface gravel.

Along the highway route there were hundreds of streams and rivers that had to be avoided or crossed with bridges. Light-pontoon companies laid floating bridges over major rivers and streams. Lesser streams that could be forded were left alone on the first push or were quickly bridged with piles and trestles. On major crossings ferries carried traffic across the river until bridges could be built.

Water was a problem in swampy areas as well. In some sections engineers had to undertake huge corduroying efforts, laying down logs that would provide passage for equipment. One such stretch ran for fifty miles between the Donjek and White rivers, where the permafrost lay only a few inches below the surface. The swampy muskeg threatened to impede progress until the army commander ordered every available hand, including cooks and clerks, to assist in laying timbers in the swamp. They did not bother cutting off the branches of the many hundreds of trees they felled but laid the trees side by side and covered them with gravel. If one layer did not do the job, another one was placed on top. Sometimes the builders had to lay as many as five layers of timbers and five layers of gravel. Corduroying was costly, time consuming, and only a temporary solution, as it would not create a permanent stable roadbed.

Pioneer roads and trails in existence at the start of construction were used to good effect. Soldiers building north of Lake Kluane had a tough winter because temperatures were the coldest on the route and no trails or roads existed. Major tasks included cutting rock near Soldier's Summit, building a pile bridge across Slim's River, and building bridges over the big glacial rivers of the Duke, the Donjek, and the White.

Gen. Bill Hoge, Highway Builder

Bill Hoge was selected by Gen. Clarence Sturdevant, assistant chief of the Army Corps of Engineers, to head the construction effort of the army engineers in February 1942. On his appointment Hoge began meeting with officials of the Public Roads Administration (PRA), the civilian government bureau charged with taking over construction once the army had rammed through the pioneer road. Sturdevant directed Hoge to link the Canadian airfields and complete a pioneer road within a year. Hoge was not given the benefit of much surveying, as he realized when Canada turned over its engineering files. "They didn't know where they were going," Hoge said. "They had this laid out purely from air photos. There were a lot of places no one had been." Later, when the American engineers got onto the ground, "they couldn't even find an Indian who'd been over parts of it," said Hoge.

Hoge planned along geographic lines. The mountains divided the route into northern and southern sectors, and he divided his forces in the same way, making his division point Watson Lake. Whitehorse was the northern headquarters while Fort St. John was the southern headquarters. Whitehorse was the obvious choice because of the tie to the White Pass & Yukon route to the coast.

Hoge took personal charge of the northern sector and of the search for the best route through the little-known country between White-horse and Fort Nelson. He spent many hours flying with bush pilot Les Cook over the passage. "I got to know the country," he said. "I also learned from the air that I could distinguish the type of soil from the type of timber on it. I could [see that] cedar always grew on gravelly ground . . . When you saw spruce, that was usually mucky and it was soft soil. You had to have something besides some gravel, and you couldn't haul gravel very far."

Les Cook showed Hoge the best place to cross the Rocky Mountains, a pass unknown to the locals but recognizable from the air. The pass, at 3,208 feet, was located eighty miles east of Teslin. Once the pass was identified, engineers on the ground surveyed a precise line between Teslin Lake and Watson Lake.

Surveying in detail was impossible during the winter, and getting more aerial surveys also had to wait for summer conditions. Intensive surveying from ground and air was carried on during the summer. The construction crews were never far behind the surveyors.

Hoge did not have as much trouble with muskeg as had been predicted. He simply rerouted the road whenever he came to a bad patch. When rerouting was not feasible, he cleared the ground and allowed the muskeg to dry out.

Hoge admitted that he did not handle permafrost effectively when he first encountered it north of Whitehorse: "I was just going to beat hell. I was making more mileage than I'd ever made. . . . I remember the spot where I had the road and everything was all right and I went back over it and it was full of water and muddy. I couldn't understand it because it had been dry before. I discovered that there was an ice lens underneath."

North of Kluane Lake, crews ran into extensive sections of permafrost, and progress slowed considerably during August and September. Hoge discovered the hard way how to tackle the problem—by corduroying. "The only thing to do," he came to realize, "was to cut timber and then throw it back on top, make a mat of timber and branches and everything else to protect it and then put dirt around that. . . . I had to put a blanket over the perma-frost . . . that finally worked, but it was considerable work."

Hoge wondered why others experienced in northern building had not advised him about permafrost. He did not think any American "knew anything" about it at the time. "Everyone talked about muskeg and everybody talked about mountains and crossing lakes and rivers, but they never heard of perma-frost, which was the worst thing we had to contend with."

Hoge believed that he was doing a great job against tough odds, but critics had a different view. Gen. Sturdevant came to be critical of Hoge's rate of progress. Hoge also had a vociferous critic in Thomas Riggs, former chief of the U.S. Canadian International Boundary Survey and former governor of Alaska. Riggs, a member of the Alaska International Road Commission, complained that the route that the PRA was building deviated so far from the army's pioneer road that two parallel routes were developing.

Corps officers decided that Hoge was inefficient and had failed to coordinate his efforts closely enough with those of the Public Roads Administration. He was fired after seven months of herculean work. Hoge was bitter. He believed that he was the victim of the personal animosity of a ranking officer who cared more for display than achievement. Fortunately, the dismissal did not hurt his career. He went on to become a successful tank commander on the European front, and at the end of the war, Hoge commanded the 4th Armored Division. In 1953 he was promoted to four-star general and retired in 1955 as commander-in-chief of U.S. Army Europe. According to highway historian David Remley, "Of all Bill Hoge's many contributions . . . none better demonstrated his abilities as a leader, organizer, commander, and engineer than his seven months on the Alaska Highway."

The Soldier Workers

Years after the war, G.I. builders recalled their participation fondly. Jerome Sheldon was one of the young American soldiers sent from Vancouver, Washington, to Skagway and then over the White Pass & Yukon Route to Whitehorse. Sheldon's detachment of the 18th Engineer Regiment started work in April 1942 on the 300-mile stretch from

Whitehorse to the Alaska border. Their base was a tent city placed on the plateau above the town, near the airport.

A few patches of winter snow still remained on the ground as the soldiers cut brush along the route in advance of bulldozers. Other squads cut pine and spruce trees for the construction of culverts and bridges. The men worked in leapfrog fashion over short stretches of the long route, clearing or bridge building, then jumping ahead of other finishing crews to repeat their specialty tasks.

The work was hard, and so were living conditions. "In our camps," Sheldon said, "we lived in 16-foot-square tents, which we struck and re-erected with each move. We heated them with tub-like, wood-burning stoves, substituting the larger, 55-gallon fuel drums converted into wood burners during winter." Cooks prepared food on portable gas ranges; the soldiers ate while standing at high tables made from trees cut nearby. The men wore broad-brimmed hats with mosquito nets in the summer, changing to fur hats and parkas with the cold. "As winter came on," Sheldon recalled, "we were still living in tents. Ice would form above our cots despite the maintenance of all-night fires. We slept in duck-down, double-layer sleeping bags."

The soldiers worked in three eight-hour shifts around the clock in snow and muck. Living in tents and eating B-rations, they had plenty to complain about, yet they did what was required.

Surveyors got a little help from aerial surveys, and then they improvised. Working with haste and without benefit of more precise surveys, they took sights from the tops of trucks or perches in trees. "Someone climbed on a bulldozer with a compass and pointed in the direction the road was to take," Sheldon said. "Thus came about some of the meandering that exists on the highway today."

Robert A. Kaye led a survey party ahead of the 35th engineers out of Fort Nelson. It was his job to make corrections in the alignment of a route that followed blazed-tree markers before the trees were pushed over by the oncoming army of Caterpillar tractors: cold, hard work. Years later, in 1983, Kaye, who had gone on to a distinguished career in transportation engineering, drove the highway with a trucker. "I could have done a better job in the alignment effort," he said, and was almost willing to argue that his wavering course had indeed been a clever scheme to fool the Japanese.

By January 1943 Sheldon's regiment was among those that were no longer needed, and his outfit was sent to the Aleutians. Sheldon did not get a chance to travel on the highway until some twenty years after its completion. Traveling by bus between Beaver Creek and Lake Kluane, he, too, heard the popular explanation of the road's crookedness: "The driver said that the Army had deliberately planned the curves so truck convoys wouldn't present a straight-line target for Japanese fighter planes. The driver's remarks, honed by repetition, were delivered with an air of authority. Not from me did he hear a contradiction."

The highway was never used for military shipping to the extent some of its planners envisioned. Most war materiel and personnel were shipped by sea transport routes to Alaska, especially since much of the traffic supported the Aleutian Campaign, and the road was too primitive to handle much freight during the war years. But the construction effort, completed on schedule, was a success and boosted wartime morale in Canada and the United States. Building such a grand project in a race against time seemed to reflect the pioneeer spirit that exemplified Americans.

Impact on Indians

The several Athabaskan Indian peoples along the highway route include the Beaver, Sekanni, Tahltan, Kaska, Tutchone, Han, Tanana, Tanacross, Tanaina, Kuchin, and Koyukon. Twenty thousand soldiers and construction workers had far less economic and cultural impact on them than one might imagine. Although some observers and some Native Americans have described the mighty invasion as culturally disruptive, neither the immediate effects nor the long-term ones can be easily categorized. There is a tendency among some writers to exaggerate the effects of the construction period and overlook the process of the previous two centuries.

Fur gathering and subsistence hunting and fishing were the chief pursuits of Native Americans along much of the corridor from earliest times. The Klondike gold rush of 1897–98 did not alter the traditional way of life, as few Native Americans were lured to mining. The buildup of communities did provide hunters with a bigger meat market, but the overall pattern of living did not change.

So, too, was the case with the highway construction. A few Native Americans took jobs as guides or laborers, but most preferred to continue their familiar trapping and subsistence hunting, particularly as fur prices were high in the 1940s.

If the economic consequences were slight, the construction did appear to adversely affect Native American health. The road opened the region to such diseases as measles, dysentery, jaundice, whooping cough, mumps, and meningitis. Flu and measles were particularly virulent, with an epidemic in 1942–43. Statistics for the southern Yukon Territory indicate a significant increase in the mortality rate for those years. The impact was all the greater because the birth rate declined during the same period and the population was a small one. Yukon Indians numbered only 1,563 in 1939, 1,531 in 1944, and 1,443 in 1949.

But it is obvious that native peoples throughout the North benefited by the increased accessibility of medical services. Before the highway, Native Americans located in such remote places as Teslin, Upper Liard, and Burwash had no easy way to get to a physician or a hospital. The highway introduced to them both certain diseases and the means to cure them.

Impact on Wildlife

Canadian authorities as well as many Alaskans suffered some alarm over the potential depletion of wild game when the American soldiers and workers were granted hunting privileges. Rumors of waste and detestation fueled anxiety over the fate of the wildlife and the Native Americans who were dependent upon it, but these rumors proved exaggerated, as comparatively few soldiers hunted.

The first steps were taken by Canada in 1942 to restrict hunting in the huge region later to be designated Kluane National Park. The restrictions, stimulated by Secretary of Interior Harold Ickes's concern for preservation in Alaska and the Yukon, had greater impact for Native Americans of that region than did hunting by soldiers. Native protests led by the well-known guide Eugene Jacquot of Burwash Landing induced the government to exclude a ten-mile-wide corridor in the White River district, but only until 1949.

The half century since construction has seen tremendous efforts in Canada and Alaska to protect and manage wildlife resources. With statehood in 1959 Alaska took over management of hunting on all lands, and officials keep a close watch on the seasonal takes. In Canada also, restrictions on hunting ensure that game is not severely depleted. The creation of national preserves and parks in both countries, including those created in Alaska in 1980, have provided further protection to wildlife.

Opening the Country: Dawson Creek to Fort St. John

Big road a-building
Hear it come
Get your pick a-swinging
For that Yukon run.
— *The Big Road*

Tony Dimond, Alaska's delegate to the U.S. Congress at the time of Alaska Highway construction, strenuously opposed the name "Alcan" for the new road. "It sounds like 'ashcan,'" he complained.

In recent years the official name *Alaska Highway* has prevailed over *Alcan*, and there have been other changes in placenames along the highway as well.

For the most part, however, historic names, where they were known, were honored by road builders. It is a pleasure to sound the many placenames. We could recite a litany with the names of the rivers that cross the highway: Kiskatinaw, Pine, Peace, Blueberry, Sikanni Chief, Bucking Horse, Prophet, Muskwa, Fort Nelson, Racing, Toad, Trout, Liard, Coal, Kechika, Smith, Dease, Rancheria, Swift, Morley, Wolf, Teslin, M'Clintock, Takhini, Alsek, Slims, Duke, Kluane, Donjek, White, Tanana, Chisana, Robertson, Johnson, Gerstle, and Delta.

Of all the names along the road I like Wonowon (Mile 101), Destruction Bay, Moncho Lake, Rancheria, Champagne, Keno, Faro, Teslin, Kiskatinaw, Soldier's Summit, Kluane, Dezadeash Lake, and Dalton Trail.

19

Of course, Indian names also abound. But you can hardly blame those who came to the country after the Indians for using some of their own names for the land and its prominent physical features. It is unfortunate that commonplace names predominate—Bear, Beaver, Salmon, Mosquito, Fish, Porcupine, Fox, Moss, Eagle, Rock, Moose, and Caribou. This similarity in names creates confusion. Indian names can also be confusing and, in translation, are usually just as banal as the whites' names. Muncho (Lake) means "big, deep water." Muskwa (River) means "bear." Dezadeash (Lake) is more sophisticated, as it describes a native fishing method unique to the area—the use of pieces of shiny white birch bark to attract fish into the range of waiting spearmen.

Off the road, in any of the mining areas, the places are named as in other parts of the mining West. You get such names as Bedrock, Quartz, Placer, Bench Creek, Coal, Bonanza, Nugget, Eureka, Eldorado, and the like.

Province of British Columbia
British Columbia is the most westerly part of Canada except for Yukon Territory. The province, with 3 million people, extends 813 miles from its southern border with the United States to its northern border with the Yukon Territory. From Alberta to the Pacific Ocean it extends 438 miles. Of this large region the Alaska Highway traverses 605 miles through rolling uplands, plateaus, and mountains to reach the Yukon border. The highway follows the eastern side of the Rocky Mountains before crossing the divide at Summit Lake (Mile 373).

The history of the province is as diverse and interesting as its natural scenery but is only treated here in reference to the highway region.

Dawson Creek's History
Dawson Creek has had a short but stirring history as an agricultural settlement, rail center, and jumping-off place to the Alaska Highway. George Dawson of the Geological Survey of Canada surveyed the area in 1879 and praised the agricultural prospects for grain and other crops. The first settlers located here in 1912, and the Northern Alberta Railroad (now the Canadian National Railway) reached the town in 1930. Until 1942 the population never exceeded several hundred; then

suddenly trains full of American soldiers and support personnel poured in to create a populace of 20,000.

The town was still booming in the winter of 1943 when a devastating fire swept through the central area, a one-block square holding two large stores, gas stations, and other businesses. Thousands of residents jammed the area to watch the firefighters, including American soldiers pumping water into the flames from an army tanker. Rumors of dynamite stored in one of the burning buildings did not worry the spectators until a thunderous explosion shook the earth. Bill Thompson, a young construction worker from Kansas, described the impact: "It wasn't so much a blast as the end of the world." He had been watching two American soldiers standing on the roof of a building: "The soldiers and the roof vaporized before my eyes. There was nothing in front of me but flames and a great, growing roar that went on and on—it seemed forever.

"For one incredible second, it was deathly quiet, with only the flames flickering. Nothing moved; there was no sound. Then the screams started in the sudden darkness."

Rebuilding of the town began as soon as the fires were doused. Forty years later Bill Thompson returned to Dawson Creek and Alaska, not having been North since he left in the spring of 1943. "I had to go. The call of the place was so strong." At Dawson Creek he saw a small, modern city, "paved, sleek and clean, with big department stores and supermarkets."

Gertrude Baskine, a Canadian writer, was the first woman to receive a military pass to travel over the highway. She arrived at Dawson Creek in July 1943 and noted the scars of the great fire of the previous February. She was amazed by the stir in the town, which was bursting with construction forces, by the piles of lumber and pipes, cylinders, and casings, and by the countless mounds of equipment. She was also impressed by the dust as the wind roared through town like a bulldozer intent upon moving the entire prairie's topsoil. The fire-ravaged place looked desolate despite the crowds of men and the bustle. Later she was driven up the highway and was thrilled to see what had been accomplished in such a short time.

Highway workers and soldiers left Dawson Creek when the highway construction was completed, but the permanent population grew vigorously because of the highway and other economic developments. New transportation links included the British Columbia rail connection, Highway 2 to Grand Prairie, Highway 49 to Spirit River, and the John Hart Highway (Highway 97 south to Prince George, B.C.), all of which made the town a genuine transportation hub. By the mid-1950s the population had reached 9,000. Petroleum and coal production in the region since then have also bolstered the local economy, transforming the once dusty, quiet village to a bustling market center. Dawson Creek's population today is approximately 12,000, but it serves an area population of 66,500.

George Dawson, Scientist and Surveyor

The town was named for one of Canada's most distinguished scientists, George Dawson. He led the party of men from the Geological Survey to survey the area in 1879. Dawson also worked in the Yukon, and his name was given to Dawson City, the great Klondike gold camp of the Yukon Territory, which was founded in 1896. Often the older northern town is called Dawson, but old-timers along the highway always refer to the latter as "Dawson City" to clearly distinguish it from Dawson Creek.

Dawson was a brilliant scientist, a man of wide scope and varied talents. Born in Nova Scotia in 1849, he suffered a crippling illness in his youth that left him dwarfed with a twisted back. Despite this handicap, Dawson earned honors as a student of geology and natural history in Edinburgh and London and won an appointment with the Geological Survey of Canada. He served on the International Boundary Commission of 1873, which marked the 49th parallel across the prairies; on the British Columbia surveys; and in the Yukon Territory.

Dawson was not an explorer in the sense of Alexander Mackenzie and Robert Campbell, two great fur trader-explorers, but because he laid the foundation for maps and investigated regional geological descriptions, he helped spearhead the developmental phase that usually follows exploration. He identified and appraised mineral and other resources of the land, estimating their value and thereby encouraging settlement.

The Peace River Block

The Peace River Block, which Dawson Creek serves, includes 3.5 million acres of arable land. In 1883 British Columbia ceded this land to the national government in exchange for financial aid in the construction of the Canadian Pacific Railroad. The CPR did not build into the Peace River Block at that time but eventually took over the Northern Alberta Railway. The national government opened some of the land to homesteading in 1912, then returned the block to British Columbia in 1930.

Mileage Designations

Mile references cited between Dawson Creek and the Alaska border are those used in *The Milepost*, the most popular guidebook available to highway travelers. *The Milepost* cites the distances from Dawson Creek and from Fairbanks and also gives the mileage as it was in 1942. Straightening of the highway over the years has made the distance between Dawson Creek and the Alaska border shorter by 32 miles. The mileposts along the Canadian section of the highway use kilometer distances. At the Alaska border the mileposts referenced here reflect actual driving distance.

Dawson Creek Station Museum

Before hitting the road from Milepost 0 in Dawson Creek, travelers may want to visit the Dawson Creek Station Museum for inspiration. The attractive museum is housed in the renovated station of the Northern Alberta Railway and is operated by the South Peace Historical Society.

For travelers interested in the construction of the highway there are exhibits and a documentary film, by Richard Finnie, made in 1942. The film is worth seeing despite the war propaganda of the narration.

For railroad buffs the station itself will have charm, as it is furnished to represent the glory days of the railroad operation in the 1930.

Other exhibits focus on significant aspects of Dawson Creek and Peace River Valley, including Native American culture, the fur trade era, government surveys by George Dawson, and railroad, telegraph, agriculture and transportation activities.

What the exhibits show is that highway construction in 1942 is only one phase of the region's history. Some of the places the highway connected had been active communities for a long time for whites and much longer for Native Americans. Visitors can look back before any human history through the museum's geologic displays.

Visitors can also prepare for some of the natural sights along the highway by looking at the wildlife exhibits in the museum. Most of the animals represented are familiar, but the museum has a huge mastodon tusk that was found in a nearby riverbank.

If you want to carry along a book of placenames, you may be able to find a copy of *Alaska-Yukon Place Names*, by James W. Phillips, but it is out-of-print and hard to locate. Another book, by R. Coutts, *Yukon Places and Names*, may be available. Northern Canada cannot boast of so comprehensive and distinguished a compendium as Donald Orth's *Dictionary of Alaska Place Names*. You can find a copy of Orth, but it is outsized and does not make a good traveling companion.

Mile 0

The traveler cannot plunge out of Dawson Creek directly into the wilderness. He must get by some major industrial plants, a few road-side enterprises, and scattered farms.

Mile 2: Louisiana Pacific Waferboard Plant

The plant, east of the highway, represents a new industry for the region. In 1987 the Louisiana Pacific Lumber Company began producing 1 million board feet of waferboard from its newly constructed mill, most of which is shipped to the states.

Mile 17.3: Kiskatinaw River Bridge

A turnoff leads to the Alaska Highway Campgrounds and the road to the Kiskatinaw Provincial Park. The two-lane paved road is a section of the old Alaska Highway and takes motorists across the unique curved wooden bridge over the Kiskatinaw River. The bridge has a curvature of nine degrees and is still in use.

Mile 30.5: Alexander Mackenzie Historical Marker

A turnout holds a historical marker honoring the great explorer Alexander Mackenzie, whose adventures and accomplishments are related at Mile 301: Liard Highway Junction.

Mile 34.4: Peace River Bridge

Getting men and materials across the Peace River caused highway builders great difficulty. The engineers put a ferry into service over the summer of 1942, but it was not able to keep up with the masses of freight. Soldiers built a timber trestle bridge in October that was smashed by the fast-flowing river in November. The celebrated Roebling and Sons Company, builders of the Brooklyn Bridge and others, was commissioned to build a steel suspension bridge.

Engineering was difficult because the water on the northern side was deep and because each spring's breakup promised the threat of huge ice chunks smashing against bridge foundations. To further complicate matters, the Pine River, pouring into the Peace just above the bridge, created a turbulence as it pushed into the east bank, then recoiled to crash into the west pier.

Foundation work started in December 1942 and was completed in March. As the river would break up in April, engineers had only a month to set up an erection tower on the river ice and assemble the sections of the 2,130-foot structure. The ice also provided the surface for all the other construction equipment. This dramatic race against time was enlivened by delays in the shipments of steel from Edmonton. As the weather grew warmer and heavy rains fell the engineers worked furiously. By April 5 they had the steel and were able to get the north tower in place. Over the next five and a half days they erected 700 tons of steel and skidded the erection tower off the ice just as the river breakup commenced. Work on the suspension cables and concrete roadway lasted until early August, when the bridge was opened to traffic. It had only taken a little over four months to build the great bridge.

The threat of ice and water, however, remained. In the winter of 1949 workers dumped some 800 five-ton boulders into the river above the bridge to block the current. Again in 1952 highway forces improvised a cofferdam with 25,000 blocks of concrete weighing 300 pounds each. Unfortunately, these measures failed to protect the piers for very long.

On October 15, 1957, residents hurried to the bridge after hearing the loud popping of steel snapping. With motorists on the highway, they watched in awe as the entire west pier began sliding toward the river. Engineers labored to shore up the pier but could not arrest its progress as it moved twenty feet nearer the water during the morning hours. The suspension wires slackened, girders fell off the pier, and the entire span thundered into the river, raising a mighty splash.

Highway travelers depended on ferries and a temporary bridge until a new cantilever and truss bridge was opened in January 1960. The new bridge does not offer the same dramatic scene that the old suspension bridge presented, but its design and construction have passed the test of time.

Mile 35: Taylor

Just across the Peace River Bridge to the north is Taylor, a community of 911 residents, most of whom are employed at the giant petrochemical, grain storage, and sawmill complex located there. The community lies on a broad, fertile plateau that impressed explorer Alexander Mackenzie favorably when he saw it in 1793. "The land above the spot where we encamped, spreads into an extensive plain and stretches onto a very high ridge," he noted. "The country is so crowded with animals as to have the appearance, in some places, of a stall-yard from the state of the ground. The soil is black and light. We saw this day two grizzly bears."

Herby Taylor, a former Hudson's Bay Company trader, homesteaded in the region in 1906. He decided that the ferry landing on the river should be identified as Taylor Flats and posted an appropriate sign. A neighbor, Robert Barker, thought Barker Flats had a better ring and removed Taylor's sign in favor of his own. The men carried on for some years, shifting signs until the government fixed Taylor as the official name.

Taylor got its first school in 1919, and the community struggled along until highway construction in 1942 gave it a boost. After the war the community languished. The *Milepost* in 1952 did not mention Taylor, only noting a "Drive-In Cafe & Garage at the north end of the Peace River Bridge." Development was foreshadowed in 1947 when natural gas was discovered on one of the Taylor farms. In 1955 the Petro-Canada Company built a gas processing plant. The Westcoast Energy natural gas pipeline runs from the plant across the Peace River on a pipeline bridge just east of the main bridge, thence south to Vancouver, B.C., and western Washington State. Upstream the Peace River has been subdued by the Peace Canyon and W.A.C. Bennett dams.

Tamed Landscape. For a distance beyond the Peace River the landscape cannot be called wilderness. Certainly wildlife has not the abundance that Mackenzie observed two centuries ago. The country seems tame and controlled, with livestock grazing on its lush meadows. A profusion of wildflowers includes the ubiquitous fireweed, which lights the way down every road in the North during the summer.

Travelers seeking something else will be restive; the very contour of the land suggests its submissiveness to man. Views from the road are not so different from parts of Alberta or Montana: soft, undulating hills, a vast sky, and views opening to a far-distant horizon. For many travelers the chance to see deer, caribou, wolves, moose, bear, and other wildlife from the highway—or on it—is the highlight of their northern travel experience. Opportunities for sighting animals increase as travelers get beyond St. John. Viewings are especially good in the early mornings, when caribou may be discovered grazing along the highway and other wildlife show less wariness than they might later in the day.

Mile 47: Fort St. John

The original fur-trading post of Fort St. John dates to 1793, making the place one of the oldest white settlements in British Columbia. The Hudson's Bay Company established a post in 1820 just before merging with its rival, the North West Fur Trading Company, in 1821. The post, named Fort D'Epinett, was closed in 1823, but another post was opened some years later.

At the entry to Fort St. John stands another Alexander Mackenzie memorial, and looming up to dominate the town is the Mackenzie Hotel skyscraper. Now there can be no doubt who the leading hero of the country is—the persistent Scot who followed the courses of two great rivers to the Arctic and Pacific oceans to open the way for further extension of the fur-trading network.

Early Days at Fort St. John. General Sir William F. Butler gave many of last century's readers some idea of Fort St. John and adjacent country in his popular book, *The Wild North Land* (1874). Butler's reconnaissance in 1872–73, covering 2,700 miles from Fort Garry on the Red River to the Rockies, brought him to the isolated post. "At the bend of the Peace River," he wrote, "where a lofty ridge runs out from the southern side, and the hills along the northern shore raise to nearly 1,000 feet above the water, stands the little fort of St. John. It is a remote spot, in a land which is itself remote. From out the plain to the west, forty or fifty miles away, great snowy peaks rise up against the sky. To the north and south and east all is endless wilderness—wilderness of pine and prairie, of lake and stream—of all the vast inanity of that moaning waste which sleeps between the Bay of Hudson and the Rocky Mountains."

Butler's expression, "vast inanity of that moaning waste" shows the attitude of people of the last century. They did not see virtue in empty wildness and longed to see some industry.

Butler stayed at Fort St. John for a few days with the Hudson's Bay Company's agent, George Kennedy, and helped the trader deal with the threat of a local man called Dan Williams. Williams believed that the trader was taking over his property and warned of a violent response. The general sided with the trader: "I clearly pointed out that murder, arson, and robbery were not singly or collectively in unison with the true interpretation of British law."

Dan Williams, an African-American, was one of the handful of early settlers. He was a survivor of a gold stampede to the Peace River in 1871. A few others remained after the first season, when the sandbars gave up most of their gold: They included Twelve-foot Davis and Banjo Mike. For the most part the scattered population lived in peace and harmony, but Williams did get into trouble a few years after his dispute with the HBC trader. Following a controversy with another man, he fired his rifle at the man's house and served three months in jail for assault. Dan then returned to his old haunts and maintained his independent ways until his death by natural causes in 1886.

William Ogilvie, Land Surveyor. William Ogilvie, the dominion land surveyor for the Department of the Interior, was another distinguished Canadian government scientist. He made a survey of the Chilkoot Pass to the upper Yukon River before the Klondike gold rush and was on hand to survey the booming gold camp of Dawson City just after the discovery of gold in 1896.

In 1891 he was at Fort St. John, which was still a quiet fur-trading post, and noted its potential. The Hudson's Bay Company trader kept a small garden "on which they raise potatoes and garden stuff together with barley and oats. The grain always ripens and the vegetables are as good as one would wish to use," Ogilvie observed.

The Hudson's Bay Company and local Indians kept horses, and Ogilvie considered it a promising aspect of the country that horses could survive over the winter. The country was milder than he expected: "St. John is visited frequently during the winter months by the so-called Chinook winds, which often sweep the snow completely."

Ogilvie, wishing to know more about the history of the country, examined the journals kept by earlier traders. The HBC required its men to keep a record of daily events, but as Ogilvie ruefully remarked, "each officer seems to have a different idea of what a daily event is, and there seems to be a want of continuity." The character of the recorders showed clearly in their records. "Some appeared to have enjoyed a quiet sit-down with a pipe and pen and had a pleasant confidential chat with a friend, narrating their own doings, and hopes and fears in connection with them." Others considered their journal an audience "to whom they grandiloquently communicated their estimate of their own powers and ability."

Ogilvie reviewed the journals for periods back to the 1860s and got a sense of the climate and prospects but advised against settlement. "I would not advise anyone seeking a home in our great North-West to think of Peace River." The area suited to farming was too limited, and distances would make living expensive. "The fur-bearing animals found in this vast northern district may truly be said to be the only source of revenue it has at present. The business of all in it except the missionaries, and they are not altogether exempt, is fur trading."

Ogilvie did not favor the independent traders who competed with the Hudson's Bay Company, arguing that "a very deplorable result of such competition is the demoralization of the Indian. He seems to consider that fur is worth anything and everything he can get for it. He seems to think that he has been defrauded in the past (I am not sure that he is often taught so) and that he is quite justified in repudiating his debts."

No one took responsibility for conserving the fur resource. Beaver had become very scarce. "It is almost too late now," Ogilvie noted, "to interfere to preserve this resource of the country."

The Beaver Indians. Hugh Savage was the first journalist from British Columbia to visit Fort St. John. In 1911 he described the trading post; the residence of Dan Williams, who earlier "created some disturbance in the valley of the Peace"; and the Indians. "The churches of the Catholic Church and the Church of England had been abandoned," he wrote, "owing to the fact that the Beaver Indian is practically impossible to deal with from a religious point of view."

Montague was the Beaver chief whose name was given to the prairie and creek beyond the fort. Earlier the trading post had been more important, Savage noted: "To it lead all the land and water trails of the north and along them for over a century has the Indian toiled, bringing in his harvest of fur." Even Dog Rib Indians from the distant Nelson River came to trade, but now fur was getting scarce and whites were coming into the country in ever-increasing numbers.

Savage noted that four government survey parties had been in the field the previous year to cut out the boundaries of the Peace River block and run baselines preliminary to dividing the land into townships, sections, and homesteads. Truly, changes were coming.

One year later, in 1912, historian-trader Phillip Godsell described the Beaver Indians encamped at Fort St. John as "this impudent branch of the far-flung Athabascan race. . . . They were untamed Indians who . . . still retained their pride of race and looked contemptuously upon the white man as very inferior people. . . . Catholic priests had tried to civilize these natives but had been driven out with insulting jeers and gestures." The Beavers were willing trappers and traders but viewed "with hatred and genuine alarm the increasing number of whites who were coming each year into their land." They considered the Peace River their southern border.

Godsell, who lived among the friendly Crees, did not like the belligerent Beavers. He believed that Beaver and Sikanni leaders had led the night attack on a party of Klondikers in 1898. The white men were encamped on a 1,000-foot hill behind Fort St. John when the Indians sent their supply-laden wagons crashing to the ravine below the camp. In justice to the Indians, they had been reacting to the shooting of an Indian horse by a white man in another party.

Warburton Pike. Of all the travelers and storytellers of the North, Warburton Pike is one of my favorites. Prior to the gold rush and the popularity of Jack London and Robert Service, the public only gradually learned about the great wilderness of northern Canada through the writings of a few perceptive travelers. General William Butler was one of them, but the work of Warburton Pike in *The Barren Ground of Northern Canada* (1892) and *Through the Subarctic Forest* (1896) is even more interesting.

Pike did not break much new ground as an explorer, but his long treks showed that with persistence, hard work, and the help of Indian guides and packers, travelers could find their way around. And, significantly, a clear-eyed traveler could discover much that was beautiful in the North.

In *The Barren Ground of Northern Canada* (1892), Pike described the region as he saw it in October 1890:

"At Fort St. John's we found Mr. Ginn busy with a band of Indians who were taking their winter supplies, and I had a chance of hearing their accounts of the wilderness to the north in the direction of the Liard River; they described it as a muskeg country abounding in game and fur, but a hard country to reach, as the streams are too rapid for canoes and the swamps too soft for horses to cross. They occasionally fall in with a small band of buffalo, but have never seen them in large numbers."

Leaving Fort St. John, Pike followed the Peace River to Hudson's Hope, which he described as "a small unpretentious establishment, a mile below the wild canyon by which this great stream forces its way through the most easterly range of the Rocky Mountains. The Indians were all encamped in their moose-skin lodges on the flat close to the fort waiting for the trade to begin, and I was surprised to hear how few representatives of the once numerous tribe of Beavers are left. It is the same at St. John's and Dunvegan, and the total Indian population of the Upper Peace River cannot exceed three hundred, an immense falling off since Sir Alexander Mackenzie first crossed the mountains by this route."

Later Pike met a well-known white resident. "Twelve-foot Davis, who acquired this name not from any peculiarity of stature, but from the small though valuable mining claim of which he had been the lucky possessor in the early days of British Columbia. A typical man of his class is Davis, and his story is that of many a man who has spent his life just in advance of civilization. Born in the Eastern States of America, a 'Forty-niner in California, and a pioneer of the Caribou Diggings discovered far up the Fraser River in Sixty-one, he had eventually taken to fur-trading, which has been such an attraction for the wandering spirit of the miner. Here among the mountains and rivers where formerly he sought the yellow dust he carries on his roaming life. There is a strong kinship between the two enterprises; the same uncertainty exists, and in each case the mythical stake is always just ahead. No failure ever swamps the ardor of miner or fur-trader, or puts a stop to his pleasant dreams of monster nuggets and silver foxes."

Pike sometimes took foolish chances in winter travel. When a chinook wind brought an unseasonal late-November warmth to his camp near Hudson's Hope, Pike could not resist a voyage into the mountains to the Hudson's Bay post of Fort McLeod (today paralleling Highway 97 from Dawson Creek to Prince George). He hoped to make a swift canoe passage before the freeze-up to the junction of the Findlay and Parsnip rivers, thus passing the highest part of the range and getting within four days' walk of the post.

Winter water passage was arduous for the Pike party. The ice was running as the men hauled their boats upriver by towline. It began to snow, which made footing along the river bank slippery. "But we got on fairly well, and were far in the heart of the mountains when we camped on Sunday night [the fifth day out] under one of the steepest and most forbidding peaks that I ever remember to have seen in any part of the Rockies.

"Monday was really cold, and our difficulties increased; the towline was sheeted with ice and three times its ordinary weight, while the channel was in many places almost blocked; poles and paddles had to be handled with numbed fingers, and our moccasins from constant wading turned into heavy lumps of ice; but we pushed on, and at nightfall had passed the mountains and emerged into a more inviting country."

Pike kept to the river despite heavy running ice and almost came to disaster in the swift current. Finally, the party landed and considered whether the better course might be a return to Hudson's Hope. Pike's guides encouraged him to keep on by foot. The men set out through the woods, encountering deep snow and heavy underbrush. After two days of travel they reached the Parsnip River, which was now frozen in a "remarkable" manner. "The first jam," Pike noticed, "had probably taken place at the junction of the Findlay; the water had backed up till it stood at a higher level than the summer floods, and the gravel beach was deeply submerged. There was no appearance of shoreline, as the constant rise and fall in the water prevented gradual freezing; jams would form and break up again, and huge blocks of ice were forced on each other in every conceivable position. Often too the ice was flooded, and it was already cold enough to freeze wet feet; the backwaters were full, and the ice on them usually under water or hanging from the banks without support; the shores were fringed with a tangled mass of willows, heavily laden with snow and their roots often standing in water, while behind, rising to the summit of rough broken hills, was the dense pine-growth of the great sub-Arctic forest."

A few days later they were out of food. They had been traveling on the river ice but had been forced to leave it when overflows made passage difficult. Pike figured that the fort was only a few hours away and welcomed an end to their journey. "When night caught us we were still in the woods, and, although there was no supper and snow was falling softly, a bright fire and the prospect of reaching the fort in the morning kept us in good spirits enough. I was one of the unfortunates without a blanket, and was glad to see daylight come again and with it a cessation of the snowstorm."

Starting out without breakfast was not pleasant. "The walking for the first two hours was very hard, through a thick growth of young pines rising among the blackened stumps and fallen logs of a burnt forest, up and down deep gullies, with the snow from the branches pouring down our necks, and our loads often bringing us up with a sudden jerk as they stuck between two little trees."

But this part of the trip was not the worst. They did not reach the fort as expected; instead they endured another cold, hungry night and set off again in the morning. After some hours the men came to the terrible realization that they were lost: They had been following the wrong river. "I fully realized the awful position we were in," Pike said, "lost and starving in the mountains with no guns to procure food, no snow-shoes with which to travel over the increasing depth of snow, and no clothes to withstand the cold of mid-winter which was already upon us."

After eating some boiled moose skin carried for moccasin repair and drinking some wild herb tea, they started downriver to the food cache they had left at the junction of the Findlay River. On the way they improvised another meal. They found a bit of flour in a sack they had thrown away as they had ascended the river. "At the same time a mouse was caught in the snow, and, with no further preparation than singeing off the hair, was cut into strips and boiled with the flour into a thin soup."

On December 17 they reached their food cache after having been virtually without food for ten days. The cache was mostly flour. They ate and rested, then were forced to wait out a blizzard. Finally they started for settler Tom Brower's cabin. It took a week of hard traveling before they reached safety, more dead than alive.

Later, Pike agreed that "it was a stupid act to leave a supply-post so late in the year, unprovided as we were with the necessary outfit for winter travelling." He paid the price on the trail and, he ruefully complained, on social occasions when "I received plenty of gratuitous advice as to what I should have done and where I should have gone from people who had never themselves been in a like predicament, and had no further knowledge of hardship than perhaps having to pay a long price for a second-rate dinner."

Edmonton Trail to the Klondike: Fort St. John to Muskwa River

Today, after nearly 50 years of continuous regrading,
the worst thing about the highway is its nasty reputation.
— B.C. *government brochure*

Choosing a milepost for the path of the Edmonton Trail along the highway is arbitrary, as the trail closely paralleled the highway over a long distance. I chose Mile 47.1 because most stampeders headed toward Fort St. John, a known place on the map.

When the merchants of Edmonton realized the potential of the great Klondike gold rush in 1897, they resolved to get in on the bonanza by promoting a route from their city. Edmonton, then a sleepy prairie town of 1,200, boomed with the Klondike news as merchants, calling patriotism to their cause, promoted an "all-Canadian," or back-door, route. The Edmonton Trail, it was claimed, would spare stampeders the rigors and expense of the coastal trails from Lynn Canal or the Yukon voyage from St. Michael. In exaggerating the ease of travel over routes from Alberta, promoters were praising a country of which little was known.

It was 1,200 miles from Edmonton to Dawson City as crows and aircraft fly, but by the shortest overland route, via the Peace River, the distance was 1,700 miles. Some argonauts preferred longer routes, including the stretch of 2,500 miles by way of the Mackenzie River, which entailed crossing the Continental Divide near the Arctic Circle.

When it comes to writing Klondike gold rush history, Canadian historians prefer to emphasize the greed, aggression, and skulduggery of Americans over those of their countrymen. But if one reads carefully such excellent books as *Klondike Rush Through Edmonton* by J. G. MacGregor, evidence of Canadian greed and incompetence can be uncovered. MacGregor tries to keep the focus on the heroics of the stampeders rather than the futility of their endeavor, hoping to give more meaning to the event.

MacGregor concedes that the yearlong procession of 1,500 Klondikers does not compare to the migration of thousands of American settlers along the Oregon Trail, but he finds no other comparable trek in North American annals. "The famous 1874 summer time march of some three hundred North West Mounted Police across the prairies to Fort McLeod, backed by the resources of the Dominion Government, was only three months and one thousand miles long. The rush of homesteaders to the Canadian West came mainly by train. The prospectors who poured in to open Ontario's and Quebec's northern mines travelled a scant two or three hundred miles. Even the Fraser River and Caribou gold-rushes swept their participants a mere three or four hundred miles."

Yet of the Klondike rush through Edmonton, one of the more foolish mass treks in history, MacGregor writes: "For magnitude, daring and adventure, this year-long migration of prospectors over routes which varied in length from 1,500 to 2,500 miles is unparalleled in Canadian history. On it youths grew to manhood, hoary heads found their graves. Twenty women faced the rigors of travelling through a Canadian winter, two babies died and another was conceived and born, even though in the remote vastness of Canada's northwest 70 lie buried or unburied, even though all but a score of the 725 who reached the Klondike returned empty handed, this trek of 1,500 outward-bound from Edmonton was not a failure but a rare chapter of courage and endurance."

In contrast to this glowing tribute, some sterner appraisals have been reported. Sam Steele of the Mounties, for instance, thought it "incomprehensible that sane men" would attempt any of the overland routes from Edmonton.

The Edmonton Board of Trade, which promoted the route, was itself seduced by the hopes of stampeders. The eager gold rushers came to the city because it was at the end of the rails at the apparent overland jumping-off place to the Klondike. Edmonton merchants saw no reason to inquire further and began advertising the glory of the Edmonton Trail. Those who knew that no real trail existed kept quiet for patriotic reasons.

What the Edmonton Trail stampeders did not weigh carefully enough were the logistics of transporting equipment and a two-year supply of provisions over a long wilderness trail. And Edmonton promoters did not bring reason to bear on the problem. Newspapers and publicity handouts attacked the efficiency of other routes, citing the crowding on the Chilkoot Pass and the Yukon River and the high passenger and freight fares from the Pacific Coast. It is hard to believe such favorable comparisons gained credence, but some prospectors were persuaded. They liked the ease of outfitting and wanted to believe the trail was one "that cannot be blocked." Promoters did concede that their trail might be long and difficult, but they argued that all routes had difficulties and challenged men to prove themselves: "The man who has not resolution and ambition and energy and good management and capital enough to carry him to the Yukon by the Edmonton route will be a great deal better off some place else."

It has been estimated that fewer than a dozen adventurers reached Dawson City by the fall of 1898, and perhaps only 100 of the 1,500 to 2,000 stampeders ever reached their destination. Many of them spent two winters on the trail; most turned back after one winter. Many died or gave way to despair. One man left a sign on a tree: "Hell can't be worse than this trail, I'll chance it," then shot himself. He was one of seventy men who died on the Edmonton Trail.

Some of the Edmonton Trail stampeders chose the route because it seemed to offer a cheap and convenient way of getting machinery needed for gold recovery to the Klondike. Inventors and promoters offered miners all kinds of untried equipment, including steam sleighs, thawing machines, and mechanical diggers "certain" to yield a treasury of gold. It was foolish to buy such machines and doubly foolish to try to transport them north. All of the mechanical follies taken on the Edmonton Trail were abandoned along the way.

Gold rush chronicler Pierre Berton noted that some of the stampeders were as picturesque as their machinery. Lord Avermore, a British aristocrat, traveled with fifteen well-bred friends, lots of servants, and five tons of provisions and equipment, including champagne, toilet paper, and folding tables for dining. Along the way several of the retinue died from pneumonia and exposure. Others were injured in falls or suffered frostbite. Dissension and violence diverted the party further until it disbanded in confusion as members fled back to Edmonton.

Three separate routes led to the Peace River and reached points along today's highway in the Fort St. John area. The shortest was the hardest, a direct westerly course from Edmonton across muskeg, swamp, empty prairie, and woods. A second followed creeks and lakes via the Swan Hills. Parties with horses lost most of their animals because forage was scarce. A third route, the northerly water route, went via the Athabasca and Lesser Slave rivers and the Lesser Slave Lake to the Peace River.

Travel conditions did not become easier once the Peace River was reached. Some of the stampeders made the dreadful mistake of angering local Beaver Indians, as did one party who either shot an Indian horse or destroyed Indian bear traps after several of the party's horses had been injured by them. Indians retaliated by charging through the travelers' camp at night, scattering their livestock and shoving their wagons over a precipice.

Few stampeders continued after reaching the Peace River, where they learned that no trail existed along the 1,000 miles to the junction of the Pelly and Yukon rivers. Edmonton merchants had hired a man named Taylor to blaze a trail, but he only managed to make slashes in trees along the way, which was a far cry from a marked trail that would accommodate pack animals. Taylor cheered on the travelers he met with false reports of "lots of gold on the Nelson" and men making "thirty dollars a day on the Liard."

The hardy ones who pushed on did not find miners digging gold; they stumbled through bogs and were forced to find their way around impassable windfall areas, where masses of dead spruce blocked progress. Horses trying to get through these obstacles bled and died. The stench of their carcasses was the best guide to stampeders following the lead parties.

At the northern tip of British Columbia the argonauts reached the Liard River, and many took to boats to follow the turbulent stream upriver, poling and portaging past Hell's Gate, the Grand Canyon, the Gates of the Damned, and Devil's Portage. Passage via Devil's Portage required an eight-mile trek over a mountain. From Liard Post on the Yukon Territory border, the stampeders moved up the Liard's tributaries to the divide that separated the Liard from the Pelly. Scarcely anyone could face trying to travel beyond the Liard. We have the complete record of only one party that arrived at the Yukon via the Peace River route, and its members were Mounties.

The Mounties as Trail Blazers

The legendary North-West Mounted Police, better known as the Mounties, had a shaky start in Alaska Highway country, as they were employed outside their constituted police activities. In 1897 the government ordered them to perform the unusual duty of blazing a trail for the stampeders from Fort St. John to the Klondike. Inspector J. D. Moodie and four constables left Edmonton in September 1897. At Dunvegan Moodie paused to round up more dogs and horses for transport. While he was waiting an American called Wilson who claimed he had been in the country since 1890 offered his services as guide to Fort St. John.. The party set off along the south bank of the Peace River on October 14, then ran into heavy timber west of Peace Coupe Prairie, where Wilson lost the trail. Moodie scattered his forces to find the trail and lost Wilson. The Mounties wasted three days looking for the guide but only found signs of his erratic wanderings. Concluding that Wilson was crazy, lost, and of no use, Moodie abandoned the search for him and moved on.

At Fort St. John, Moodie dallied for a month, waiting for more dogs and not showing much resolution despite the practical necessity of moving along before winter snows. To provide future dog feed he killed several of his worn-out horses and dried their meat. Finally, he fired the guide he had hired in Edmonton and employed some Beaver Indians. The way was hard, and Moodie quarreled often with his guides. Along the trail he had to shoot several more faltering horses and use their meat. By the time the party crossed to the western slope of the Rockies they were relying entirely upon dogs for transport. On January 18 the Mounties reached Fort Grahame on the Findlay River, where Moodie set up winter quarters.

He kept busy traveling around the country as far as Quesnel and gathered supplies there, but it was mid-July before the trailblazers got going again. By this time Moodie realized that he was not much help to stampeders, many of whom were making better progress and using other routes, but he was always pleased to meet parties who had given up and were returning. In August Moodie reached Lower Post, then moved on to the vicinity of today's Watson Lake by way of the Liard River. From there he headed up the Frances River, followed the west arm of the Frances Lake to the Finlayson River, reached Finlayson Lake, and on September 30 began running down Campbell Creek toward the Pelly and Yukon rivers. On October 24 Moodie reached the well-known country at the mouth of the Pelly River and so ended his trip. He returned to his post at Maple Creek, Saskatchewan, in only eighteen days.

According to historian J. G. MacGregor, in *Klondike Rush Through Edmonton*, "Moodie was a Mountie and probably a good one who, when directed to carry out a mission, went and carried it out. During his rapid trip back to Maple Creek he must have wondered why he had been ordered to take packhorses, dogs and canoes, to slog his way through deadfall timber, up or down cascades and over un-travelled passes for thirteen months to blaze a trail to the Yukon when by conventional means he could make the reverse trip to the prairies in eighteen days."

MacGregor could not forbear a small biblical joke in summarizing Moodie's task: "Nevertheless, he had blazed the trail he had been sent to mark, and, like his long-dead biblical predecessor, Joshua, the son of Nun, and Caleb, the son of Jephunneh, he had searched out the land and reported on it, listing the streams to be bridged, the side hills to be graded, the areas of good pasture, and a host of other information, and in due course compiled all of it into a good report.

"Unlike Moses, to whom Joshua and Caleb had reported, Moodie's superiors filed his report and forgot it."

The situation had changed. No longer was there a desperate need for a road. Signs indicated that everyone who wanted to reach the Klondike had arrived and few were likely to use an Edmonton route even were a road to be built.

In his report Moodie expressed his confidence that he had chosen the best route, going via Fort Grahame, "the only practical one . . . not even known previously by the Indians." But he acknowledged his reservations as well: "With regard to the usefulness of this trail as a route to the Yukon, I should say it would never be used in face of the quick and easy one via Skagway and the White Pass; but on the other hand, I have not the slightest doubt that if the country were opened up and thoroughly prospected it would be found immensely rich.

Almost every stream yields colors, and it only requires that these streams be followed up and properly prospected."

As it took Moodie one year and one month to reach the Yukon River, he effectively demonstrated that his way to the Klondike was of little use. Most stampeders used a more direct route and made better progress than did the police trailblazers, but the Edmonton Trail in any variation must be judged among the major fiascos of the gold era.

Mounties as Road Builders

Police authorities were embarrassed by Moodie's failure to open up a good route to the Klondike, but they probably did not beg for another exploration or road-building assignment. Nonetheless, they were given another chance to shine a few years later when a second transport scheme was launched. Authorities in Ottawa ordered the Mounties to build a road from Edmonton to the Yukon River. The government's commitment of a small force of police showed little understanding of the magnitude of the road-building task.

In March 1905 thirty-two men with sixty horses set out for Fort St. John, the point at which they would build their road. After building quarters at Fort St. John, they cleared an eight-foot-wide wagon road fifty-four miles to the west, including laying logs over marshy areas and building rest cabins at thirty-mile intervals. By September 1907 the police had built 377 miles of trail west from Fort St. John to the Yukon Telegraph Trail 104 miles north of Hazelton.

Historian–fur trader Phillip Godsell praised the effort of the small contingent of Mounties, who "attempted with nothing but guts, brawn and axes to emulate [sic] the work done later by the thousand United States Army troops with modern bulldozers and mechanical equipment." According to Godsell, the government quit the project when the British Columbia government refused to share the cost of pushing the road beyond the Stikine River: "It became the Road to Nowhere, the project was discarded, the Fort St. John barracks were abandoned," and the Mounties, ragged, trail worn, and weary, returned to their base at Fort Saskatchewan wondering at "the weird ways of politicians."

Godsell and other pioneers of the country had reason to deplore the government's lack of resolve in stopping the job, but to maintain, as Godsell did, that the road was "near completion" was a gross exaggeration. To complete a usable wagon road the government faced enormous costs, and it concluded that the amount of trade and populace in the country did not warrant the necessary vast expenditure.

Mile 50.6: Charlie Lake

An early tragedy during the 1942 highway construction occurred when eleven soldiers drowned after their truck broke through the ice on Charlie Lake. Several other soldiers, including the two lost in the Dawson Creek fire, died during construction, and some memorials to them still exist along the highway.

In the 1950s travelers could stop at the Charlie Lake Hotel, Garage, and Store and enjoy beef raised by the proprietor on a lakeside ranch. Today there are a store, a pub, an RV park, a gas station, and as a sign of the economic trends, an office of the Ministry of Energy, Mines and Petroleum.

Mile 53.7: Junction with Highway 29 to W.A.C. Bennett Dam and Hudson's Hope

The W.A.C. Bennett Dam, built in the mid-1960s, is one of the largest earth-filled dams in the world. Waters backed up behind it form the huge Willistone Reservoir. In 1990 a new tourist center was opened at the dam.

Before the building of the Hart Highway, the road from Mile 53.7 only continued 53 miles to the Hudson's Hope coal mines. Now it continues west and south from Hudson's Hope and the dam to connect with the Hart Highway (Highway 97) at Chetwynd.

Mile 101: Wonowon

Wonowon was the site of a construction highway control center during the construction era. The community of 150, including gas stations, motels, stores, restaurants, a pub, a post office, and a campground, was formerly known as Blueberry for the Blueberry River to the east.

The aptly named Wonowon must be kept in mind during the rest of the trip, because beyond this point the highway mileage differs from that of the original road, which has been improved and straightened over the years.

Godsell's Trail. Phillip Godsell made the next serious effort at trail building in 1925 under orders from the Hudson's Bay Company. Godsell blazed what he called "the first link in the Alaska Highway," making a rough trail from Fort St. John to Fort Nelson that covered a distance of about 300 miles. To accomplish his work he defied local Beaver Indians, who resented the venture. He heard that a Beaver Indian had threatened to shoot the first white man who crossed the Sikanni Chief River, the border of the Beaver hunting grounds. "I didn't lightly brush aside [this threat]," Godsell said, "since I knew of old the activities of Chief Bellyfull and his former partner, Wolf. Only a few days before they had shot up the post at Fort Nelson and thrown Fred McLeod, the factor, into the river."

Nonetheless, Godsell pushed on, "fording mountain torrents, leading our pack-horses knee-deep through miles of gripping muskeg, fighting alternately droning clouds of pestiferous mosquitoes and angry wasps that rose from the moss beneath our horses' feet to sting their bellies and convert them into bucking demons."

One motivation for Godsell's trail work was the appearance of free traders in the region who threatened the hegemony of the Hudson's Bay Company in the fur trade. The Lamson and Hubbard Company of New York had put diesel riverboats into service to reduce freight rates and, for a time, gave the Hudson's Bay Company spirited competition. The high cost of transport had always determined the price of goods brought in for trade.

Godsell described Fort St. John in 1925 as a "marooned settlement atop a plateau," the only sign of commercial activity in "a country as lonely and isolated as ever." By this time the long-hoped-for railroad had been extended to Grand Prairie but was not expected to ever get beyond Dawson Creek.

Eventually Godsell and his helpers reached Fort Nelson, 236 miles from Fort St. John by today's highway. He called it "one of the loneliest and most isolated trading posts in the entire Northwest." Two traders lived there, maintaining five log buildings, and considered themselves lucky if they got two mails a year.

"In the surrounding forests," Godsell said, "Slavey and Sickannie Indians hunted bear and moose, and trapped lynx, mink, fox and marten which they bartered for knives, food, gunpowder, and cloth." Prices were ten times higher than outside. "So costly was transportation that a hundred-pound sack of flour sold for forty dollars, bacon at two dollars a pound, tea three dollars; sugar, prunes and other dried fruits at a dollar a pound, while gasoline—when the factor could spare it for the outboard motors of one or two up-to-date trappers—was considered cheap at four dollars a gallon."

Godsell's place in pioneer highway history should be respected, even if his trail did not revolutionize transport in the North. It was improved over the years, and army engineers were pleased to utilize it in 1942, although they found higher ground above the low, swampy Godsell route for their highway.

Mile 143: Pink Mountain

The elevation here is 3,600 feet. A community of 100 people has developed who provide services to tourists, sports enthusiasts, and travelers.

Mile 144.7: Beatton River Bridge

The Beatton River was named for the trader Frank Beatton of the Hudson's Bay Company at Fort St. John. Historian Godsell described him as "a grizzled and hard-headed Orkneyman" so loyal to the company that he refused to make a courtesy call on the *Diamond P*, a riverboat put into operation by a rival trading company in 1912. Beatton was always wary of the local Beaver Indians, particularly one named Wolf, who had tried to stab him in the back after being refused credit.

Mile 156.2: Sikanni Hill

During construction, Sikanni Hill was better known as Suicide Hill. The grade was perilously steep, and accidents were common. Even after the highway was opened to civilian travel, Suicide Hill remained a menace until considerable work moved the road westward, reduced the grade, and eliminated a nearly right-angle turn at the bottom that terrorized drivers. Before these improvements were made, someone has posted a sign at the top of the grade: "Be prepared to meet thy God." Regulars on the highway were accustomed to seeing scenes of destruction at the bottom.

A bit of Robert Service–style verse, "My First Trip up the Alaska Highway," by Eugene Wilkinson, captures the driver's terror as he survives one seven-mile grade on Suicide Hill, then reaches the top of a second grade:

"But my gaze of wonder turned to awe as I started down the hill,
For there lay the battered twisted form of a tanker cold and still."

Suicide Hill was the most notorious place on the highway but not the only place of danger. Drivers taking corners and twists in the road at high speeds often crashed. Dust obscured vision in the summer, and ice made the road treacherous in the winter. Until the 1970s the maintenance department posted ominous, blood-red signs at dangerous places that held such messages as "4 KILLED HERE."

Some people profess to feel sad about the straightening of the highway, but the benefits of the work can be measured in a number of ways. Consider the costs of maintaining the original stretch of highway on its uncertain foundations over the years and the risks of driving on slippery ice around countless blind curves, and give thanks.

It is part of the singularity and charm of the Alaska Highway that travelers still discuss the condition of the highway at every rest stop. Increasingly, the exchanges of information seem less vital as the Alaska Highway swiftly approaches standards that are familiar elsewhere. Yes, something is lost. Drivers will be less comradely, less likely to help you repair a flat tire, but everyone will live longer and with more serenity.

The Truckers of the Highway. The drivers of freight trucks on the highway have always had a certain pride in their work. Historically, they have complained about auto and RV drivers, whom they call pilgrims, but they have usually been quick to respond to any driver's emergency. They are always in a hurry and determined to pass loafers, who in the days before paving would then eat dust for a time. Thus pilgrims do not always speak well of the truckers, either. Many stories are told of truckers who, after finally passing slow drivers, have stopped long enough to block the road, get out, and bang the offending auto with a wrench or, to stress the importance of using the rear view mirror, pulled it off. But since most of the highway has been paved the two classes of drivers have had less cause for conflict.

Truckers do not shut down their engines on overnight stops in cold weather. Travelers may encounter a whole yard full of parked behemoths puffing and rumbling through the night. If they are parked near your motel window, your dreams will not be sweet.

Mile 159.2: Sikanni Chief River Bridge

The ruggedness of the country prior to highway construction is illustrated by events of the winter of 1941, when a Caterpillar train reached what was called Sikanni Landing or Sikanni Cache. The train carried construction equipment from Dawson Creek for work on the Fort Nelson airport and was led slowly along by a trail-breaking bulldozer. The construction Cat train included ten sleighs with twelve-foot runners and an eight-foot spread pulled by a D7 Cat. After the bulldozer cleared the way, the Cat pulled five of the sleighs forward, then went back to bring up the other five sleighs. Breakdowns and accidents slowed progress. Just going down Sikanni Hill took three days of tedious effort. The expedition spent from February to April getting to Sikanni Chief River, all the while bulldozing, clearing, blasting, and making bridges. At Sikanni Chief River the construction crew waited for breakup, then moved the equipment by barges on the Sikanni Chief and Nelson rivers to Fort Nelson. In all, the trip took four months.

Mile 159.4: Sikanni Chief

A lodge and RV park are located here. Motorists can see the original highway bridge to the west. It is one of the few remaining original bridges along the highway, although it is not in use.

Mile 173.1: Bucking Horse River Bridge

North of Fort St. John the traveler finds the scene he has been looking for. The farmlands disappear and dense forests crowd the road in places, then open to reveal spectacular views of distant ridges of the Rockies. What variegated colors the mountains offer! Where do those shades of purple come from? If you draw close, they will vanish before your eyes. What compels us more—the color and dominance of distant mountains or the sense that we must reach above for something?

On my last drive down I saw a wolf hurry across the road in the early morning. The place of wolves in our culture is curious. Nature writer Barry Lopez and others have pointed out how people have created their own image of what wolves are, one fashioned by fear, superstition, and ignorance as much as any rational consideration of the beast and its relationship with human communities.

Foxes are more common than wolves along the road. They are beautiful animals that almost seem capable of outracing any car as they dash across the highway.

Mile 176: Trutch Mountain

Mile 176 is the southern end of the 28-mile, 45-km bypass that avoids Trutch Mountain, named for an English civil engineer who was the first lieutenant governor of British Columbia. Until the highway was rerouted in 1987, travelers climbed the mountain, an outreach of the Rockies that reaches an elevation of about 8,000 feet. Climbing to the pass at 4,000 feet was hard on automobiles but rewarding to scenic viewers. The beauty of the region is described well by Edward Mc-Comb, who saw it in 1968:

"Spaciousness. For once it would seem that the Almighty had at his disposal enough room and materials for the execution of his most grandiose design. Further south the mountains are often crowded closely together as tops pinch in the valleys; sometimes they hang right over our heads and shut out the sky and make breathing difficult. . . . We see the materials of creation displayed in a flawlessly balanced design: a great valley with a river winding through it; a forest of splendid trees spreading away on either side of the river and far up the nearest mountain slopes; here or there an open field or meadow interspersed to break the monotony of forest green; and far off, forming the perfect backdrop, a range of snow-capped mountains."

So often our literary descriptions of mountains are based on summer views. What McComb would have seen during the winter would have given quite a different impression. For all its beauty snow has a way of canceling variety, smoothing over and filling in the shadows and textures of summer. Snow may glisten in the sun, but it also obliterates color. In winter the beauty is countered by a sense of waste. Nothing grows or lives in the plant world in that cold, sterile season. Where is the fruitfulness, the smiling, benevolent side of nature?

Mile 217.2: Turnoff to Prophet River Provincial Park

From this point the highway parallels the Prophet River to its junction with the Muskwa River, just south of Fort Nelson. The Prophet River was the point reached by the famous Bedaux expedition in 1934, another pioneer demonstration that northern British Columbia was hard country before the Alaska Highway existed.

The Mysterious Charles Bedaux. Charles Bedaux, a Frenchman who became an American citizen, was another pioneer of the Alaska Highway route. He was supremely confident of his ability to pioneer a road to Alaska and had induced the provincial government to expend $600 toward the exploration of unmapped areas and to allow a government surveyor and geographer to accompany him.

His venture in 1934 excited great interest because of his extravagant style. Bedaux was a wide-ranging sportsman and traveler. He had made trips to northeast British Columbia in 1926 and 1932. In 1930 he crossed the Sahara Desert in an automobile—a half-track Citroen, going 10,000 miles from Mombasa to Casablanca.

The governor of Alberta and other dignitaries saw the Bedaux Sub-Arctic (Citroen) Expedition off after a parade in Edmonton on July 6. With five vehicles and lavish equipment Bedaux expected no difficulty in conquering the long stretch of mountainous wilderness across British Columbia to the Alaska Panhandle.

Canadian newsmen were dazzled by the princely excursion, which included fifty family members and retainers, including Bedaux's wife and her maid, his gamekeeper and valet, a mechanic, a Swiss alpine guide, a radio operator, and a Hollywood cameraman and assistant. Awesome, too, were the expedition's equipment and supplies, including such luxuries as pâté de foie gras, canned Devonshire cream, smoked Scottish salmon, champagne, and silver cutlery. In addition to the tractors Bedaux had hired 130 packhorses. One carried nothing but French novels; another had room only for the shoes of the women of the party.

Bedaux found the going harder than he anticipated, even in Alberta. The mud of the Peace River Valley threatened to swallow his expensive vehicles. By the time the expedition got to Tupper Creek, British Columbia, the tractors needed repairs. The rough trails continued to tax the machines, and Bedaux did not reach Fort St. John until July 17. But the leader was not discouraged. He had previously arranged for three advance parties, using pack animals, to go ahead of his machines. The first advance party took to the field on April 30 to construct a tractor trail beyond the Prophet River.

Bedaux's expedition moved at a snail's pace. The half-tracks could not make it on steep slopes without the help of animals and men. Bedaux abandoned the machines, pushing on with horses. Progress remained slow. The lack of forage was an obstacle, as were the huge quantities of baggage. Bedaux moved northwest from the headwaters of the Muskwa River, along the Findlay River, north to Sifton Pass and where the Laird-Findlay rivers divide. By this time the horses were in wretched shape, starved, suffering from hoof rot, and exhausted. Shooting them was a mercy; giving up the expedition was a necessity.

Bedaux abandoned or gave away most of what he had carried to the wilderness, returning by boat on the Finlay and Peace rivers. The venture had cost over $250,000. Folks just laughed or shook their heads over Bedaux's folly until World War II, when Bedaux became infamous. Reportedly, he was close to ranking German officials and an adviser to France's puppet Vichy government. Bedaux undertook a mission to the Sahara to investigate the possibility of bringing oil to the German war machine by pipeline. When the Allies invaded North Africa in 1943, Bedaux was arrested. He was in Miami awaiting trial for treason in February 1944 when he killed himself. Bedaux's notoriety encouraged suspicion among those who reflected upon his earlier jaunt along the Alaska Highway. Had that supposedly frivolous voyage been a German plot to seize a vast western territory? It seems unlikely, but it does add a piquant touch to the pioneer trek of Charles Bedaux.

Mile 281: Muskwa River Bridge

At Mile 281, formerly 296, the Muskwa River bridge signals the lowest elevation on the highway—1,000 feet. The road between Trutch Mountain (Mile 176) and the Muskwa was once well known for its twists and turns as it weaved through the heavily forested alluvial soil seeking a sense of direction. The original highway took a tortured course in this and some other stretches. The army engineers, desperately hurried, followed the line of least resistance to avoid the deep muskeg pits into which Caterpillars might fall.

The 1943 Flood. In June melting mountain snow often causes floods of the Muskwa River, which are worse when rains are heavy. A heavy flash flood in 1943 caused the river to rise twenty-eight feet in twenty-four hours and sweep away the army's storage tanks. Boats and barges that could be secured in time were tethered to the tops of trees along the bank. As the water receded the thick mud made movement of men and vehicles almost impossible until the ground dried. Another big flood in 1956 almost equaled the rise in 1943. Most years the floods threatened to take out the bridge because the river carried masses of trees that had been uprooted by the swiftly moving water. Men moved swiftly to dynamite log masses jamming the bridge before the structure was knocked down. The construction of a new bridge with higher clearance and better-designed piers in the mid-1970s reduced the threat.

Bears. In Athabaskan, *muskwa* is the word for bear, and many black bears live in the region. Quite naturally folks pause at the Muskwa

50 _____ *Passage to the North*

River to recall the best bear stories they know. Over the years bear stories have become more sophisticated. During highway construction, favorites included that about the tired worker who kept kicking the cot of his tent mate to stop his snoring until he discovered to his terror that a bruin occupied the bunk.

A better story to retell at Muskwa concerns a man named Walker, who wanted to make an overland hike in the upper Muskwa River country but dreaded meeting a ferocious grizzly. He was amazed to learn that hunters were not encouraged to destroy these menacing beasts on sight, that killing bears in or out of season was not considered a public service. A friend told him that the best way to avoid trouble was to imitate a bear in all his movements. Bears were easily flattered and would not attack a man friendly enough to imitate them.

Walker set off on his journey and soon had an opportunity to test the imitation theory. He was bending down to drink from a brook when he saw the reflection of a grizzly in the water. He almost had a heart seizure. The bear was a towering monster, all fangs and claws, the very stuff of horrible nightmares.

Walker remembered the strategy he had planned and did not panic. The bear, which had also been drinking from the brook, stood up. Walker stood up, The bear raised his deadly paw and scratched himself. Walker raised his hand and scratched himself vigorously, smiling at the bear to express his good feelings. The bear then stepped behind a tree. Walker knew what that movement meant, but an imitation of this call of nature was not timely. "Too late, old fellow," Walker called cheerily. "I've already done that."

A favorite modern story holds a touch of irony. Two hunters were outfitting to hunt caribou in this region and heard that a mad grizzly had been seen. The hunters, close as brothers, figured they could handle the bear in some way. Joe laughed, though, at Jim's preparations. Jim replaced his boots with a new pair of expensive running shoes. "Hell, man," Joe said, "don't you know no better than to think you can outrun a bear?"

Jim smiled. "What makes you think I have to outrun the bear?"

The pair were never very close after this episode.

The Mountains Rise:
Fort Nelson to Muncho Lake

A thousand miles from nowhere
A thousand miles to go
How long how long
    Nobody seems to know.
                     — The Big Road

The Rocky Mountains form the predominant physical feature of a good part of the long route from Dawson Creek to Fairbanks. From north to south in the Rockies there runs a continuous series of peaks and ridges that form the Continental Divide. Rivers on the eastern side flow to the Gulf of Mexico, the Atlantic Ocean, or the Arctic Ocean. Rivers to the west flow to the Pacific Ocean.

Peaks seen from the highway are not so high as those in the Colorado Rockies or those of the dominion parks at Banff and Jasper. The range varies greatly in its extension from the Brooks Range of Alaska with its modest 5,000-foot peaks to the lofty Sierra Madre Oriental of eastern Mexico.

Fire and Ice
The gradual uplift of the Rockies began as long as 60 million years ago, eventually raising towering domes of granite and schist. Where the rising rock domes fractured, outlets were formed that allowed magma to pour out of the earth's interior. Rising central cores caused the buckling of sedimentary beds thousands of feet thick, which had

51

been deposited by the inland seas that periodically encroached on the area. Other changes followed as the sedimentary rocks folded together, then buckled to form hogbacks. Ten million years ago another uplift began and may still be in progress, promising further dramatic changes.

But uplift and magma flow only produced the basic shapes of the mountains. The next stages of their development involved shaping or sculpturing caused by the movements of glaciers. Effects varied widely depending upon the local movement of ice sheets and the duration of ice-field covers. According to Peter Farb in *The Face of North America* (1963), the sculpturing in the West took a different form from that in New England, where ice sheets covered the mountains. "The glaciers of the west were not part of the continental ice sheet; rather, they were local valley glaciers, which originated near the heads of mountain valleys but never reached the lowlands." Valley glaciers, Farb noted, moved along like slow rivers, cutting valleys, pouring over precipices, and sometimes breaking up into deltas. The glaciers ground and polished the bedrock over which they flowed. "Every time the ice encountered an obstruction, these rocks would be turned over and polished from another angle. As a result, numerous huge boulders of the Rockies resemble a many-faceted shape of a cut diamond."

Glaciers sometimes merged with others to form larger ice masses as they moved down valleys. In reaching lower, warmer altitudes their advance slowed and melting began. Such pauses in movement led to the forming of moraine, which dammed the valley, and to the formation of lakes behind the moraines.

In contrast with the changes brought about by comparatively gradual glacial action, earthquakes and volcanic eruptions caused explosive upheavals. Conditions vary greatly over the region reached by the highway. Maps of the last great ice age, for example, show that most of interior Alaska was free of ice while Canada lay under the ice sheet.

Shaping Forces
Erosion, whether caused by winds or waters, is also a powerful force in shaping mountains. The changes caused by erosive forces are not always subtle. One area accessible to the highway where erosion can be investigated is at Stone Mountain near Summit (Mile 373). Travelers can visit the Wokkpash Recreation Area of British Columbia,

where erosion pillars (called hoodoos) stand as high as 100 yards and form walls of gorges in stately lines of up to three miles in length.

Another interesting geological feature along the highway is the lava outcrop visible at Riverdale, a suburb of Whitehorse on the east side of the Yukon River. Just below the dam is the Plino-Pleistocene Miles Canyon lava outcrop. The basalts are riddled with vesicles—holes made by gas bubbles escaping during the rocks' molten stage. Over time the vesicles filled with mineral deposits carried by ground water circulating through the basalt. Such fillings include radiating tufts of aragonite crystals and white grapelike clusters of calcite, along with dogtooth calcite crystals and brownish-yellow olivine.

Drainage Patterns

There is evidence of much shifting in the Yukon drainage basin, which occurred when the Cordilleran ice sheet, moving from the east, and the St. Elias ice sheet, moving from the southwest, overlapped during the Pleistocene glacial advances. As a result of the overlapping in the Whitehorse vicinity, glacial ice dammed the Yukon and other rivers and created lakes. A major rearrangement of the drainage patterns was the result. Glacial lake deposits of layered silt are visible today in the Whitehorse area river bluffs on either side of the Yukon River.

Geologists have figured out that until 1.8 million years ago the upper Yukon River made a shortcut to the sea by following a 189-mile route through the Takhini-Dezadeash Valley, out to the Alsek River, and through the coastal mountains to the Gulf of Alaska near Yakutat. This access to the sea was blocked as the St. Elias ice sheet formed during Pleistocene times to fill the Alsek River Valley. Ice remained in the mountains long after it had melted in the lowland interior near Whitehorse. Since the blockage, the Yukon has been forced to take its long 1,300-mile route to Norton Sound on the Bering Sea.

Rocks and Minerals

The Whitehorse Copper Belt can also be found in the Yukon Valley in the Whitehorse region. The valley is four miles wide at this point and bordered on the east by a long ridge of Upper Triassic limestone called Grey Mountain. A part of the Lewes River group, this limestone is related to a sequence of Mesozoic volcanic and sedimentary rocks that underlie the Whitehorse trough. To the west Cretaceous to Tertiary granodiorites intruded on older Lewes River group rocks, and the molten granite rocks reacted with the limestone to form skarn minerals and deposit copper minerals.

Chief ores of the region include chalcopyrite and bornite along the eighteen-mile belt between Cowley Lakes and Porter Creek. A variety of other metallic and nonmetallic minerals are also evident. Klondike miners noted the copper outcrops during the gold rush and eventually mined the ore, which was then shipped to outside smelters via the White Pass and Yukon Railway.

The Takhini River geology is varied. Ten miles north of Whitehorse the highway leaves the Yukon Valley for the Takhini Valley. Mesozoic granodiorites of the Boundary ranges of the Coast Mountains form the peaks to the south. On the north side of the highway are late-Tertiary quartz monzonites of the miner's range. There are also deposits of sand and gravel on the lower slopes of the mountains, remnants of the shoreline of a glacial lake that existed in the Pleistocene era, when glacial ice covered the region. Evidence indicates that only a few mountain peaks rising over 6,000 feet reached above the ice sheet. Travelers can also notice deposits of stratified silt and a white layer of volcanic ash in road cuts and riverbanks.

At Champagne (Mile 943.5) the highway follows a four-mile ridge, 100 to 200 feet high, of sand, gravel, and boulders formed by a retreating glacier at the end of the Ice Age. More recent erosion is visible, too; a mantle of sand dunes caused by winds reworking the older glacial sediments. The Alaska Highway cuts across this moraine.

As the highway runs north from Haines Junction (Mile 985) it enters the Shakwak Valley and extends along it for 150 miles to beyond the White River. In the valley the bedrock changes from the Mesozoic granodiorite of the coast ranges to the Jurassic schist, gneiss, and amphibolite of the Kluane formation. The St. Elias peaks are reminders of the Denali Fault, which separates the younger St. Elias Mountains to the south from the older rocks of the Yukon Plateau to the north. The Shakwak Valley appears to be the result of vertical rather than horizontal fault movements of the Denali Fault. The valley walls are fault scarps bounding a block that dropped during Pliocene times; the southwestern fault continued moving, so that modern streams cut 300 feet deeper than those in the northeastern wall. The valley was later mantled with Pleistocene and more recent deposits of till, gravel, sand and silt, and volcanic ash.

The Denali fault movement may go back to Cretaceous times, when rocks of the Wrangellia terrane in the Kluane ranges were deformed into tight folds and metamorphic banding. Stresses about 15 million to 30 million years ago probably caused the faulting.

Mile 283: Fort Nelson

Fort Nelson got its start in 1805 as a post of the North West Fur Trading Company. The traders and their families — eight men, women, and children in all — were killed by Indians in 1813, and the post was burned. The Hudson's Bay Company established another post in 1865. This post was destroyed by a flood in 1890 and rebuilt on higher ground.

Few whites lived in the region until the highway was built, but there were some pioneer attempts to improve transportation. According to local historians, it was not Phillip Godsell who built the first leg of the Alaska Highway in 1925, but Joe Apsassin, a Cree, and a white trapper named Glen Minaker. They labored in 1919–20 to improve a 325-mile-long pack trail 175 miles from Fort St. John to Sikanni Landing and 150 miles to Fort Nelson. It was 1936 before the town got its first regular mail service.

An old-timer recalled the travails of movement that existed until the highway was built: "In the spring of the year they would come to the Sikanni with teams; they had warehouses there, and they would build scows or barges, all out of whipsawn lumber, and after the ice went out the freight would be loaded and floated down on the scows to Ft. Nelson. . . . Most of the HBC freight came by river from Ft. Simpson. . . . Our people tried to get their heavy freight in during December or January. It was not unusual for heavily laden teams to break through the ice."

Mrs. Genevieve Clark, a Mountie's wife, was one of the few white women in the community in the 1930s, but whites and Indians lived in harmony. There was always plenty of work and visitors showed up most days. Trappers would call for a visit; Indians would stop by for medicine.

Army engineers who arrived at Fort Nelson in 1942 called the place Mile Zero because they were starting the road to Whitehorse from there. In time 2,000 soldiers were based at Fort Nelson, and things changed fast. Lodema George, the postmaster and storekeeper, was accustomed to receiving mail once monthly; suddenly planes flew in every day with 20 sacks. "What in the world am I going to do?" she asked. Fortunately, the army handled all the mail, so she did not have to expand immediately the six-foot space in the store devoted to it.

Earl Bartlett arrived at Fort Nelson on an electrician's job in 1943 and remained there the rest of his life. He photographed hundreds of picture-postcard scenes of the highway from Dawson Creek to the Alaska border. Over years of driving the highway, he probably came to know it as well as anyone else. By 1979, at eighty-two years of age, he had sold over a million picture postcards to travelers and was known as Mr. Alaska Highway to his neighbors.

After construction most of the soldiers were transferred, but a substantial base remained in operation for highway maintenance until 1946, when the Canadian army took over.

When traveler Iris Woolcock visited Fort Nelson in 1947 to have a flat tire and a faulty starter repaired, the place had the dismal look of a temporary military camp. In those days a traveler was relieved to see even so unlovely a settlement, but Woolcock said she felt sorry for the women and children who were part of the community of military personnel and civilians operating the air base.

Harry Dickie, local Indian chief from 1970–76, regrets the passing of the old ways with the highway's completion: "The Indians were well off; independent . . . fur sold was almost pure profit . . . their only needs were tea and tobacco. They didn't have to work hard, no pressure, no stress, not the feeling among people there is now. If there was a storm, you stayed home . . . didn't have to watch the clock or calendar . . . or wait for a cheque. The change came too quick . . . overnight with the highway. The money, the people, the liquor . . . it takes years to adjust. We have to slow down."

Most Fort Nelson Indians are Slaves, an Athabaskan-speaking people who migrated to the district in the late eighteenth century from Great Slave Lake. They lived on the river by Old Fort until they were required to move into a reserve near the highway in 1959. By 1962 most of them had moved, but the people did not like the poor garden soil, the proximity to the town, and the loss of the river environment. Mary Loe, who resisted the move until 1969, described the sorrow it caused: "It was just awful . . . people were crying . . . thought it was the end of the world. . . . They were used to the river. They were part of the river. . . . it was a drastic move that changed their lifestyle, and some never drank at all until the move."

The town's big boom came with the start of airfield construction in 1941 and the highway the next year. Development and population gain have continued with developments in agriculture, timber production, and petroleum. The natural gas–processing plant was built in 1964. Gas is sent south over an 800-mile pipeline. The railroad was extended from Fort St. John in 1971. Lumber and sulfur in pellets are among the products shipped south by rail and truck.

Highway Communities. One of the great pleasures of driving the highway is in the near-absence of towns and tawdry commercial strips that make traveling through more-populated areas of the United States and Canada an ugly experience.

Towns that you do encounter in the North are not conspicuous for their beauty. They usually have a temporary, hurried look about them, as if builders, pounding and sawing away in September, felt snow in the air and gave new meaning to "jerry-built." Jerry-built—hastily built of cheap materials—applies equally to white towns, such as Fort Nelson, and to Native American villages, even though the relative costs of construction vary widely. Growth in the last twenty years has transformed Fort Nelson and Fort St. John from mere wide places in the road to sizable communities, but it has not necessarily made them more alluring as seen from the road. There are, however, attractive areas where residents can enjoy the grand scenery. From parts of Fort Nelson, for example, superb views show the great forests of the central plain approaching the eastern bulwarks of the Rockies.

Highways have always gone between populated places, but on the Alaska Highway you sometimes sense that the community exists only to service the highway. Living on the highway strip is certainly a sweeter, cleaner experience than in times past, since the pervasive cloud of dust is almost gone. Once folks living on the highway tasted sandy grit whenever someone said "summer." Old-timers of Fort Nelson say that people took their lives in their hands on some days just crossing the road, guessing from the absence of engine noise rather than seeing that the coast was clear of traffic.

Mile 301: Liard Highway Junction

From Fort Nelson the highway veers west toward the Rockies, twisting through wild regions for some 200 miles. Travelers keen to follow fur-trading history may take the Liard Highway north to Fort Liard, Fort Simpson, and points beyond in the Northwest Territories.

Alexander Mackenzie. Traders of Mackenzie's North West Fur Trading Company established Fort Nelson in 1805, reaching the place by way of the Mackenzie River to Fort Simpson, thence up the Liard and Fort Nelson rivers. The post was named to honor the great English hero Admiral Horatio Nelson, who had just defeated the French in the grand naval battle of Trafalgar.

There is no greater name in North American exploration history than Alexander Mackenzie, the Scottish fur trader who made two epic river voyages—one to the Arctic, the other to the Pacific Ocean. The first of these in 1789 provided him with an opportunity to investigate the Liard River region and led eventually to the establishment of trading posts there. Mackenzie was a member of the North West company, the great rival of the Hudson's Bay Company until they consolidated.

On June 3, 1789, Mackenzie set out by canoe from Lake Athabasca with high hopes of finding a river route to the Pacific Ocean. By this time Yankee traders from New England ports were making long circumnavigational voyages to China, including stops for fur trading with Indians along the Northwest coast. Traders of the North West company and the HBC realized that an efficient expansion of their trade required access to the fur-rich regions of the Northwest coast.

Mackenzie knew all about the Russian fur empire based in Alaska and carried with him some rubles for trade. His party, in several canoes, included four French Canadians and a number of Indians, including an important man known as the English Chief. Soon Mackenzie moved onto the Slave River and on the second day out passed the mouth of the Peace River flowing in from the west. The party spent several days on the Slave River, portaging often, and on June 9 reached Great Slave Lake, where they were forced to remain for a week because of heavy ice in the lake and high winds. Three weeks after arriving at the lake they finally found the outlet to the river, which Mackenzie ardently hoped would lead him to the Pacific. The river, of course, was the Mackenzie.

Mackenzie pushed his men hard, fearing that his provisions would not last and that he might not be able to reach the Pacific and return before the onset of winter. They usually started out by three in the morning, toiling until late afternoon, bothered by the cold, rain, and plagues of black flies and mosquitoes.

On July 1 Mackenzie noted that "they loaded and push'd off at a quarter before 4 A.M. . . . At one o'clock there came on Thunder, Lightening, Wind and Rain, which ceased in about ¹/₂ an Hour and left us wet to the Skin as we did not land." His journal went on to record "great quantities of Ice along the Banks of the River. Landed upon a small Island where there were the Poles of four Lodges, which we concluded to have been Crees, upon their War Excursions by appearance 6 or 7 years since. This course for 15 Miles then W. where the River of the Mountains falls in from the Southerd. It appears to be a large river upwards of ¹/₂ Mile over, at the Entry. About 6 miles further a small river from the same Direction, this course 24 Miles we landed opposite to an Island the Mountains to the Southerd in Sight, as our Canoe is very deep laden and that we are in daily Expectations of coming to the Rapids, which we have been made to dread, we hid 2 bags of pemmican in the opposite Island which I expect may be of Service to us in time to come, tho' our Indians are of a difft. opinion, they having no Expectations of coming back here, this Season, of course it will be lost Close by are two Indian Campments of last Years by their way of cutting the wood they must have had no Iron works. The Currt. was very strong all Day the Indians killed 2 Swans."

The "River of the Mountains" Mackenzie met was the Liard; the smaller river was the Martin. Because his course that day, which covered 100 miles, was northwest, Mackenzie still believed that he was progressing toward the Pacific. But in paddling on the next day he saw foreboding signs. Now the party was drawing closer to the Rockies, and it looked as if the great range might be a barrier to the Pacific. What they saw we now call the Mackenzie Mountains.

On July 3, the river now coursing due north, Mackenzie halted to climb a towering hill for a view of the land ahead. Surrounding hills obscured the long-range view. "Between the Hills are Nos. of small Lakes upon which we could perceive many Swans, the Country appeared to be very thinly wooded, a few Trees of the Pine and Birch, and very small in Size, we were obliged to shorten our Stay here on account of the Swarms of Muskettoes that attacked us and were the only Inhabitants of the Place."

Mackenzie voyaged on, watching for signs of Indians from whom he might learn something of the lay of the land. On July 5 he saw the smoke of campfires and landed at an Indian camp. Most of the Indians fled at the party's arrival, but eventually the English Chief managed to persuade some less timid souls to talk with them. The Indians were Slave and Dogrib. "We made them smoak 'tho it was evident they did not know the use of Tobacco, we likewise gave them some grog to drink, but I believe they accepted of those Civilities more through Fear than Inclination by the Distribution of Knives, Beads, Awls, Rings, gartering, Fire Steels, Flints and a couple of Axes, they became more familiar than we expected, for we could not keep them out of our Tents, tho' I did not observe that they tryed to steal anything from us."

This historic encounter between Indians of the Alaska Highway region and fur traders followed the pattern familiar to other parts of the West. The traders always wanted two things from Indians—their knowledge of geography and, looking ahead, their willingness to hunt furs for them. In this case Mackenzie did not gain his immediate need. The Indians were ignorant of local geography but assured the travelers that their task was all but impossible. They attempted "to persuade us that it would require several winters to get to the sea, and that old age would come upon us before the period of our return," Mackenzie said. "We were also to encounter Monsters of such horrid shapes and destructive powers as could only exist in their wild imaginations." If this news was not discouraging enough, the Indians claimed that on the river ahead of them were two impassable falls.

Mackenzie could not be deterred by such warnings, but the English Chief and his men were upset and begged to return. Mackenzie dissuaded them and then persuaded one of the local Indians to join the party as a guide.

The traders were not much impressed by the physical appearance of this small group of Slave and Dogrib Indians. "They are all an ugly meager ill made People particularly about the Legs which are very clumsy & full of Scabs by the frequent roasting of them to the Fire," Mackenzie noted. "Many of them appear'd very sickly owing as I imagine to their Dirty way of living. They are of the Middle Stature & as far as could be discerned thro' Dust & Grease that cover their whole Body fairer than the generality of Indians, who inhabit the warmer climes."

In describing the Indians so unfavorably Mackenzie was not exaggerating to show the superiority of his own people. Great variance existed among the western Indians in appearance and cultural level.

Many interior tribes showed the results of very hard lives, including periodic famines and constant harassment by other Indians.

Mackenzie does show a more general religious and social bias in commenting, albeit humorously, upon the nakedness of the men: "Their want of Modesty & their having no Sense of their Nakedness but from the Cold would make a Person think that they were descended from Adam, and probably had he been created at the Arctic Circles he would not have had occasion for Eve, the Serpent, nor the tree of Knowledge to have given him a Sense of Nakedness."

On July 7 the traders reached the rapids they had been warned about and found they were not so bad. Mackenzie's guide deserted him, but downriver he found Indians who were able to provide him with useful geographic information. By this time Mackenzie realized he had failed to find the river coursing to the Pacific, having taken observations that showed he was much farther north than he had suspected. Bitterly disappointed, he nonetheless resolved to follow the great river to its end.

"It was evident that these waters emptied themselves into the Hyperborean Sea; and though it was probable that, from the want of provision, we could not return to Athabasca in the course of the season, I nevertheless, determined to penetrate to the discharge of them."

On July 14 the men reached the end of their journey, saw whales, and observed the tidal movement. Mackenzie left formal records of his discovery. "This Morning I fixed a Post close by our Campmt., on which I engraved the latitude of the Place. My own Name & the Number of Men with me & the time we had been here."

That date, momentous in Europe as the day the mob stormed the Bastille, was of great importance to Britain and Canada as well: Mackenzie's monument on the Arctic shore gave those countries a claim to a vast region.

Food was no problem on the return journey. The men killed plenty of caribou, birds, and fish. On July 23 Mackenzie found some yellow wax that he recognized as petroleum, but the discovery did not seem too important at the time. On July 27 he met local Indians who described a great river to the west and what seemed to be a Russian fur-trading post near its mouth on the other side of the Rockies. Mackenzie could no longer take such rumors seriously, as the speakers could not support their tales with sound information on passages across the mountains. All too often they discredited themselves by spinning wild yarns about fearsome, winged people beyond the mountains whose very looks could kill.

On the long return voyage upriver Mackenzie stopped for the pemmican cache he had left and stopped, too, where the Liard River came into the Mackenzie. Continuing east he reached the mouth of the Peace River on September 11, then crossed Lake Athabasca the next day and reached Fort Chipewyan to complete a journey lasting 102 days and 3,000 miles.

Mile 287.9: Former Radar Site at Historical Mile 304

Historical Mile 304, which refers to the milepost before highway improvement, was the site of a radar installation from 1957–64 and is now a golf course. Four miles north is Historical Mile 308, where the American army construction camp and the Public Roads Administration camp as well as housing units and a hospital were located during World War II. After 1946 many of the buildings were moved to other sections of town, and most are still being used.

Mile 333: Steamboat Mountain

The approach to the mountains is abrupt beyond the Liard River. Instead of slowly rising foothills you see huge, mesalike uprisings fronting the towering peaks of the main range. One of them is Steamboat Mountain, so called for its peculiar shape.

Mile 333.7: Steamboat Mountain Road

A narrow road off the highway lets travelers ascend Steamboat Mountain for views of the mountains and the Muskwa Valley. Along the highway at Mile 342.8 and Mile 345 are other places to view Indian Head Mountain, "a high crag resembling the classic Indian profile," and other imposing formations.

Mile 351: Dangerous Curves and Slides

Road signs warn of the dangerous mountain curves in the area of Historic Mile 368, which was called Mud Hill during the construction era. Engineers labored long to stabilize this hill, piling great masses of stones on the downhill side, hoping to support the bank. Soon after workers placed the stones, they watched them roll down into the valley below. Next they drove fifty- to sixty-foot piles that had been roped together against the embankment. Before long the sliding hill threw all the piles down into the valley. The problem seemed to be one of excessive moisture in the glacial silt. Workers removed the timber from the top of the hill and built a drainage system that eventually stabilized the spot.

Mile 373.3: Summit Lake

The highway follows the Tetsa River, which rises near Summit Lake in the Rockies. Summit Lake, at 4,250 feet, is the highest point on the highway. Descending, the highway follows the beautiful, turquoise-colored Toad River to the west.

Mile 376: Erosion Pillars

Some of the geologic features of this mountainous area, including the famed hoodoos, or erosion pillars, of the Wokkpash Valley, have been discussed in the introductory essay on geology at the head of this chapter.

To the north the highway enters a rocky sandstone gorge.

Mile 382.2: Mining Road

At this point there is a trail to the abandoned Churchill Copper Mine. Harris Davis and Bob Keays, two Fort Nelson men, discovered copper in the area of the Racing River in 1965 and operated a small mine until it closed in 1970. The Churchill Copper Mine in the same area was a larger operation that opened in 1970 but closed in 1975 because of declining copper prices. At its peak the Churchill Copper Mine employed 210 men.

Mining history of the North has not been as well recorded as in the southwestern states and other regions. There are hundreds of abandoned mines about which we know little except that the prospects of wealth induced a considerable investment.

Mile 404.6: Toad River

The highway follows the Toad River westward along the fringe of a gravel flood plain, then jogs northward over a low pass into the Trout River watershed en route to Muncho Lake, which lies between the Sentinel and Terminal ranges of the northern Rocky Mountains.

The Toad River Lodge was built in the late 1940s by Lash and Dennis Callison, two brothers, who ran the lodge with the help of their wives and were well-known hunting guides in the region. The Toad River is rich in wildlife, including Stone sheep, grizzly and black bears, moose, and caribou.

Mile 410.6: Geological Point of Interest: Folded Mountain

On the mountain face, some rock layers appear to be folded. This notable rock formation is known as Folded Mountain.

Mile 423.1: Heading North

The highway heads more directly north from this point.

Mile 424.1: Peterson Creek Bridge

Peterson Creek Bridge No. 1 was named for Pete Peterson, a local trapper who helped on the highway construction.

The Mighty Liard: Muncho Lake to British Columbia

I have often wondered that any human being
should live in a cold climate who can find
room in a warm one.
                            — *Thomas Jefferson*

Robert Campbell, an important name in Liard River history, was a Scottish fur trader who first opened up much of the highway country for the Hudson's Bay Company. In 1835 Campbell was put in charge of the HBC post of Fort Liard. Campbell, who had been with the company since 1830, was active until 1871 and traveled much of the region for the first time. With the help of arctic explorer John Franklin and traders John Bell and John McLeod, Campbell determined the geography of a large part of northwestern Canada.

In 1837 Campbell volunteered to establish a new post at Dease Lake after another HBC man failed at the same assignment. The other trader had fled the place after succumbing to an unfounded rumor that the Russian traders in Alaska had sent a large war party of Indians to wipe out the intruding British traders. From Dease Lake Campbell explored to the west and determined that the Pelly River, discovered on an 1834 expedition led by the HBC's McLeod, was actually the upper Yukon River. On the Stikine Campbell met a party of Tlingits from the coast and gathered information on the trading pattern. The Indian chief, Shakes, was a powerful figure because he

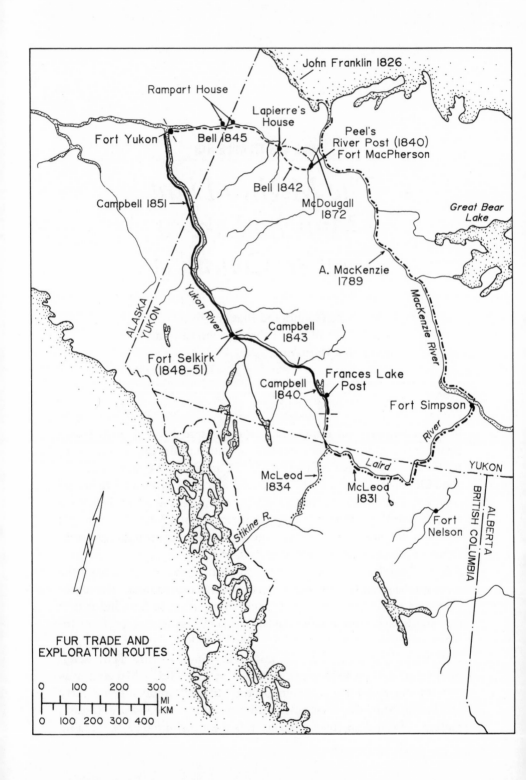

FUR TRADE AND
EXPLORATION ROUTES

controlled the flow of Russian goods from the Russian-American post at the mouth of the Stikine. Shakes and his men carried the much-sought-after Russian goods into the interior, exchanged them for furs gathered by interior Indians, then took the furs downriver to the Russians. As Campbell knew, Governor George Simpson of the HBC coveted the upper Stikine River trade dominated by the Russians through Shakes.

Campbell was astounded by the size of Shakes's camp and his numerous followers and was fearful that Shakes might resent his presence. Shakes greeted the trader like a brother, even offering him a drink of whiskey. Campbell, a devout, teetotaling Presbyterian, "merely tasted" the drink, not about to be debauched by Indian firewater.

The Indians were carousing mightily, and Campbell and his men feared a disruption of the harmony. "I was well armed," Campbell said, "having pistols and dirk in my belt, and a double barreled percussion gun, which was a great source of wonder to them as the only guns they were familiar with were single-barreled flint locks. Shakes wanted me to fire so that he might see how the gun went off. Fearing this was only a ruse to render my gun harmless, I took the precaution to have ball, powder & cap in my hand ready to slip in immediately after firing a shot. At every report, the whole camp yelled, clapping their hands on their mouths at the same time, & the noise was frightful."

Campbell remained in the camp for some hours, "the object of much curiosity till at length getting clear of Shakes and the crowd on the plain in safety (which was more than I expected when I first went among them)." Leaving the Indian camp, he rejoined his men, who had been observing at a distance, and indulged in a formal ceremony: "I forthwith hoisted the HBC flag, & cut HBC and date on a tree, thus taking possession of the country for the Company."

One of the more interesting experiences Campbell had among Indians involved another encounter at Shakes's camp. He met "the Chieftainess of the Nahanies who commanded the respect not only of her own people, but of the tribes they had intercourse with." It was, as Campbell recognized, unusual among North American Indians for a woman to hold a position of power. "She was a fine looking woman above the middle height and about 35 years old," Campbell observed. "In her actions and personal appearance she was more like the Whites than the pure Indian race. She had a pleasing face lit up with fine intelligent eyes, which when she was excited flashed like fire." Later the Chieftainess interceded to save the lives of Campbell and his men from threatening Indians and to provide food in a time of need. Campbell acknowledged: "To the kindness and influence of the Chieftainess, we owed much on more than one occasion; in fact in all probability we owed our lives to her more than once."

Campbell established a post at Frances Lake in 1842, then explored the Pelly and Lewes rivers, determining that they were actually part of the Yukon River. He confirmed his speculations by reaching the HBC post, Fort Yukon, at the confluence of the Porcupine and Yukon rivers in 1851.

Campbell established another Yukon post at Fort Selkirk and aroused the anger of the Chilkats on the shore of Lynn Canal. The Chilkats used the Chilkoot Pass, later to be the famous Klondike gold rush route, to go into the interior to exchange Russian and other trade items with interior Indians, and they resented the HBC's interference with their monopoly. In August 1852 a Chilkat war party of 27 men attacked the post, expelled Campbell and his men, and burned the place down. "The roaring and yelling of these painted fiends, smashing everything that came their way – and firing – beggars description," Campbell wrote.

Mile 436: Muncho Lake

Muncho Lake, taken from the Indian word for "big, deep lake," is remarkable for its deep green and blue tones, attributable to the leaching of copper oxide. The lake, surrounded by limestone peaks reaching 7,000 feet, is regarded as one of the loveliest lakes on the continent.

The area was opened in 1942 by U.S. Army engineers who were seeking a way around the Grand Canyon of the Liard River. Because of washouts in 1943 the Public Road Administration, which took over roadwork from the army engineers, was forced to relocate the road originally out through the steep cliffs above the lake. The highway was then built along the lake shore.

In 1974 heavy rains destroyed twenty miles of highway and undermined several bridges. Until repairs could be completed, traffic had to be held up. The same rains also closed the Stewart-Cassiar Road, so southbound traffic was held at Watson Lake. Most travelers were forced to sleep in their vehicles, and restaurants ran out of food.

More than one traveler in the old, dusty days has reached this point and, for a time, refused to go further. What could be more beautiful? they ask. What's the point of enduring more unpleasant miles on this horrible road? Judging from the smallness of the settlement in the area, such travelers have eventually become satiated with the scene, recovered their sense of purpose, and pushed on.

Every type of nature offers its own kind of appeal. Mountain gorges thrill and terrify; distant snowy peaks inspire the imagination. But lakes surrounded by mountains whose slopes glisten with cascading streams in a season when the foliage is green and profuse evoke an ineffable tranquility. So it is with Muncho Lake.

Edward McCourt, a perceptive traveler of 1968, saw in the stillness of the lake "a serenity which today is hardly ever found in places of great natural beauty, for wherever he goes man takes his noises and distractions with him." This traveler did not expect to make a return visit to Muncho Lake, and he was just as glad, fearful that when the highway was paved, "Muncho will swarm with our kind and be ringed about with offices for our housing and provisioning and pleasuring."

The traveler's fears reflect anxiety over change and deep suspicion that our fellow humans lack the sensitivity with which we are so richly endowed. Thoreau reflected gloomily on this point long ago: "It appears to be a law that you cannot have a deep sympathy with both man and nature. Those qualities that bring you near to the one estrange you from the other."

It should be noted that McCourt's fears of tourist swarms from twenty years ago have not yet been realized.

Mile 471: View of Liard River

Northbound travelers get their first glimpse of the Liard River at this point, and the highway follows the river north all the way to Watson Lake. The Liard is a tributary of the Mackenzie, which flows into the Arctic Ocean. Army engineers in 1942 found in the river a natural route to the North and cleared a passage along it.

Mile 476.6: Liard River Bridge

The Lower Liard River Bridge is the only suspension bridge left on the Alaska Highway, now that the original Peace River Bridge has been replaced.

Earlier, drivers along this stretch had to be wary over what was a twisting, up-and-down course and, in summer, a dangerously dusty one. Even now you must be attentive to the road, even though the scenes are tempting. The highway runs along the river to Fort Nelson and beyond to the British Columbia–Yukon border but does not give any views of the Grand Canyon of the Liard. Hell's Gate, the aptly named entrance to the 40-mile-long Grand Canyon, struck terror in the hearts of explorers and fur traders who ran the river in canoes. The suspension bridge crosses the river just below Hell's Gate.

The most significant historical events associated with the Liard River predate the bridge. The river was a highway, albeit a perilous one, of great importance during the fur trade era, the Klondike gold rush, and at every other time of movement through the region.

Mile 477.1: Liard Hot Springs

A short turnoff from the highway brings up one of the greatest amenities of this or any other highway. Liard Hot Springs is a place of refreshment to weary travelers who can enjoy either of the two hot springs within the park.

Some bathers find the smell of the hot springs unpleasant, but its sulfurousness is the result of its origin. Hot springs are created when water dissolves minerals from fractured faulted rock. The rocks from which the springs emerge are hot because of their depth in the fiery bowels of the earth. The hot water that reaches the surface has the odor of sulfur, which is often found near hot springs.

It was once thought that a tropical setting surrounded the hot springs. Government geologists and others who knew the rigors of the northern climate doubted the existence of this pleasing geographical aberration, but until Charles Camsell of the Geological Survey thoroughly explored the fabled "tropical valley" in 1935, the myth persisted.

Camsell had first seen the springs in 1898 and again in 1899; only in the 1920s were other visits recorded, including that of trapper Tom Smith and his daughter, who lived there for two years. Smith was later drowned in the Liard River. Camsell described the region, dispelled the notion of any tropics, and praised the hot springs. Until 1942 there were few visitors to the remote bathing place. But the springs have been used regularly since the U.S. Army engineers cleared the brush and provided access during the construction of the Alaska Highway.

Liard River Traffic. Fort Liard was part of the company's Mackenzie River district, which extended along the length of the Mackenzie River to the Arctic coast and from the east of Great Slave Lake to the border of Russian America. It also included much of northern British Columbia and the northern Peace River region. Thus the Liard River was the natural waterway for the trade of the huge region, but a none-too-reliable one. Travel on the Liard was full of perils. Trader James Anderson once reported to his superiors that "you can hardly conceive of the intense horror the men have, to go up to Frances Lake [the headwaters of the Liard]." The horrors included the rapids of the river, along which several men drowned, and the isolation of such posts as Dease Lake, where other traders had starved to death.

But, despite its dangers, the river was a highway—the only one available—and had to be used. The exploration of the river in 1887 by Canadian geologist R. G. McConnell made the Liard less mysterious, but no less dangerous.

Mile 495: Anton Money's Silver Discovery

Earlier travelers on the highway used to hear wonderful stories from the proprietor of one of the Muncho Lake lodges. Anton Money knew the country as few other men did and could describe his discovery of silver in 1926 at a spot just 1,500 feet off the highway.

Money had served in the British army during World War I. With the peace he craved another kind of adventure. As with countless other youths, he had been enthralled by the literary North of Robert Service and Jack London. Who can guess how many young folks were stirred by Service's ballads and London's stories and motivated to live in the North? Money was one of them and he secured employment with the Hudson's Bay Company.

In May 1923 he arrived at Telegraph Creek, 165 miles up the Stikine River from Wrangell, on the shallow draft riverboat *Hazel B No. 2*. It had taken the boat three days to work its way up the river, yet it could make the return voyage in a mere ten hours. As the boat was the first of the season to arrive, the whole community stood on the banks to welcome the twenty passengers aboard.

The young man, still in his twenties, was thrilled at everything he saw and rich with expectations for his future: "This was the North, Robert Service's land of abysmal loneliness, vast and untamed and beautiful, stretching away into endless distances of mountains and valley, river and lake, with places of solitude where no human had ever walked. Men spoke of traveling on the rivers for days or even weeks on end without encountering another person. How strange that seemed to one accustomed to the short distances of Europe, where a journey of a few hundred miles could take you out of one country, across a second, and into a third."

The Cassiar region had experienced a minigold stampede in 1923, and the young immigrant from England soon left the HBC for independent prospecting. He and a partner searched the region and made a long voyage in 1926, venturing eastward, poling a boat up the Liard River. It was hard work, but the men were young and optimistic. Surely they would find gold if they tried hard enough.

One day, at a lunch stop, Money did a little prospecting around the area. He found a boulder four feet in diameter that seemed to be solid ore. "Breaking chunks off with the pick the strong odor of sulphur came again and streaks of high grade galena banded the boulder like stripes on a tiger." Money and his partner grew excited. He climbed a steep bank where a landslide had recently torn off chunks of surface gravel and overburden and found more chunks of the same rock. At the top the vein was exposed. It was over four feet in width and showed heavy galena mineralization in bands four and six inches wide across the vein.

The material looked like quartz except that it was too heavy. The prospectors decided that it was probably barite with a small silver content. "To attract a mining company," Money concluded, "the silver content would have to be up in the hundreds of ounces per ton, even then it seemed doubtful that anyone would look at a four foot vein so far from transportation."

Later the partners discovered an even more precious commodity near Frances Lake—gold. Writing about it many years later he could convey the sense of excitement: "On a nameless creek, in what seemed at that moment a place a million miles from civilization, the dream of every prospector had come true for me. I had found the eternal treasure. I do not believe that any man to whom that has happened can tell others what the feeling is like. Unless you have made a strike you cannot understand the magic of the words. An old-timer once told me that when it happened to him his heart started to pound and he felt the hair rise on the nape of his neck as if a grizzly had poked its head out of the brush and looked him in the eye at arm's length. For me it was as if a cord that had been tied around my heart had suddenly been broken."

Money liked to tell the story of his gold discovery to visitors at his hunting and fishing lodge, but he also enjoyed telling about his silver ore discovery to those who considered the region remote even though they were able to drive down a modern highway. Remoteness, of course, is a relative matter.

Money had other good stories to relate of his adventures and told many of them in articles for the *Alaska Sportsman* in the 1960s and later in a memoir, *This Was the North*, published in 1975. Money prospected for mining companies in the Yukon and British Columbia until World War II shut down mining activities. It was fitting that Money, as a pioneer, participated in the great wartime construction effort. He supervised twelve dog-team crews surveying the Canol pipeline, then helped build the airports at Whitehorse and Watson Lake.

After the war Money did other kinds of work, including a stint as engineer on the Santa Barbara campus of the University of California. The North drew him back in 1952, when he built the Village Inn hunting and fishing lodge near Muncho Lake, which he and his wife operated until his retirement in 1964.

Writing of his youth, Money recalled, "I can close my eyes and still see the beauty of Frances Lake and the mountains around it. I remember the savage rapids in the canyon of the Liard and the Frances, the Christmas caribou that licked salt from my hand, the log cabins I built, my dogs and the soft whisper of a toboggan over snow. I remember the fun and ecstasy Joyce and I found by ourselves, in the solitude of the remote wilderness—the silence of the winter nights, the terrible cold of seventy-five below. I can even remember and can laugh at the poling boat and the whipsaw and the hard rips under pack.

"The North I came to from England at twenty-two was a land of untamed splendor. The mountains and the rivers, the summer heat and winter cold, the hard work and solitude taught me lessons I could have learned in no other school on earth. It fulfilled my every dream and transformed me from a green cheechako tenderfoot into a self-reliant woodsman, skilled in the things a man must know to survive by himself in a vast and harsh world."

Writing in his old age in California, Money affirmed, "The North still lives—bright as a nugget inside me."

Mile 514.2: Coal River Bridge

The Coal River region shows the impact of glacial movements in past ages in its many lakes, great gravel beds, and other surface signs of erosion. The river got its name because lumps of coal can be found along its banks and on sandbars.

Mile 524.2: Fireside

At this point the ravages of the 1982 burn known as the Eg fire are visible. The devastating fire, the second largest in British Columbia history, destroyed 400,000 acres of timber.

Mile 567.9: Contact Creek Bridge

Contact Creek Bridge is named for the meeting on September 25, 1942, of the construction crews working west from Fort Nelson with those pushing east from Whitehorse. While the official ribbon-cutting ceremony marking the completion of the Alaska Highway was held at Soldier's Summit (Mile 1,029) near Kluane Lake on November 20, 1942, Contact Creek was the first meeting place.

Mile 568.3: Historic Marker on Yukon Territory

The highway crosses the British Columbia–Yukon Territory boundary here, although some miles farther the road crosses back into British Columbia. A sign indicates, among other facts about the Yukon Territory, that it was named for the Indian word *Youcon,* or "big river."

The Yukon Territory extends from the Arctic Ocean to British Columbia and has its boundary with Alaska along the 141st degree parallel. Within its large area of 186,300 square miles there are only 25,000 people, two thirds of whom live in Whitehorse. The territory was created in 1898 as a consequence of the Klondike gold discovery in 1896, which was followed by the stampede of thousands of hopeful argonauts in 1897–98.

Mile 585.3: Hyland River Bridge

The Hyland River was named for Frank Hyland, an early trader on Telegraph Creek on the Stikine River.

Mile 598.7: Lower Post

Lower Post is at the confluence of the Liard and Dease rivers. It was once an important Hudson's Bay Company post and Indian village because of its location. A short gravel road off the highway leads to the site, but nothing historic remains. A field office of the B.C. Forest Service is located here.

Author Warburton Pike described the country near Lower Post as he saw it in 1890: "Standing on the bank of a river whose source is unknown, and with a stretch of country lying to the northward several hundred miles in length and breadth, on which the white man has never set his foot, the Liard Post may be regarded as one of the best starting points for the exploration of the North-West that are still open to the enthusiastic traveller."

Most people, Pike said, knew nothing of the Liard River, but "it is one of the most important features in the western water system of Canada. Rising, like the Peace, far to the westward of the Rocky Mountains, it cuts through the main range, and, after a wild course of some 800 miles, falls into the Mackenzie at Fort Simpson, mingling its waters with those of the Peace, the Athabasca, and innumerable smaller streams that drain the huge Mackenzie basin."

Pike doubted that the Liard could be navigated. "There are several bad canyons in the upper part of the stream, while the lower river is still worse, and has always enjoyed the reputation of being the most dangerous piece of water in the whole of the Hudson's Bay territory. It was by this route from the Mackenzie that the posts at Fort Halkett, Dease Lake, Frances Lake, and Pelly Banks were supplied fifty years ago; but there were so many disasters from boat accidents and starvation, besides the great cost of keeping up the posts, that the route was abandoned; so that of late years there has been but little intercourse between the two sides of the mountains."

Pike traveled in January with Métis guides and dogsleds from Lower Post to Frances Lake, where he wanted to establish his mining camp. In moving four sleds loaded with provisions, the dogs were indispensable, but conditions were not easy: "The travelling with heavy loads was slow, as we had to go ahead every day to break the road through the snow, and wait until the night's frost hardened up our tracks before the dogs could pull the sleighs. In the soft snow we could make no headway at all, but sometimes we found long stretches of glare ice which helped us greatly. A good deal of time, too, was taken up in hunting, as, unless we killed moose, we had to fall back on our loads of provisions that were intended for use many months afterwards."

It took a week to cover the forty-five miles north of Lower Post to the point where the Dease River flowed into the Liard River. The weather grew cold, down to sixty-eight degrees below zero. When Pike left his companions for a fruitless moose hunt, he failed to account for the dangers of the intense cold: "I had eaten nothing since early morning, and had been sweating while running after the moose, always a bad thing to do in cold weather, as you are sure to get chilled as soon as you stop for a minute."

He did not find his companions where he had expected to and panicked: Instead of remaining at the rendezvous and building a fire against the cold, he left his rifle and pack and set out on the run to search for his men.

"I could never get warm again, although I had still ten miles to go; and my nose and cheeks were rather badly frozen before I saw the glare of the camp fire through the trees." Greatly relieved, Pike reflected that a man should never try to travel alone in such conditions. "If he meets with an accident severe enough to cripple him, or gets wet by breaking through a weak spot in the ice, he is absolutely certain to freeze to death unless he is very quick in lighting a fire. In any case he should always carry an axe on his belt and plenty of matches, so that he may still have a chance if dry wood is close at hand. One of the greatest dangers lies in the fact that your fingers are likely to freeze, or at least become useless for lighting a match, as soon as you grasp the handle of an axe and impede the free circulation of the blood, as a layer of ice is sure to have formed between the moose-skin and the inside lining of your mittens. This sort of weather is good enough for travelling straight ahead on a good road with light loads on the sleighs, but in this case our dogs were overloaded, and the snow was so soft that we could not keep warm while travelling slowly."

Mile 605.1: B.C.–Yukon Border Again

The point-of-interest sign south of one of the several spots where the highway crosses borders provides a historical sketch of the Yukon Territory. The sign, while acknowledging that the region was explored in the 1840s by Hudson's Bay Company traders, slights historical occurrences over the following half century: "The territory, which was then considered a district of the Northwest Territories, remained largely untouched until the Klondike gold rush, when thousands of people flooded into the country and communities sprang up almost overnight." Road sign authors should not dismiss history so readily: Indians and whites were there hunting, exploring, simply trying to survive.

Notice that as you move north from Fort Nelson the scenery is of wooded valleys and far-off mountains. Even at a distance the mountains offer a variety of color with variegated tints of mauve, gray, and sandy hues. Sunny blue skies and green forests add to the enchantment. In this lovely land history was made as men of diverse races struggled in their different ways to keep body and soul together in a region that sometimes, as Robert Campbell admitted, seemed a "horrible place."

Yukon Country:
Watson Lake to Whitehorse

Start from Canada
Go way up past Tanan
Glory road building
Called the Alcan.
          — The Big Road

"Cold, eh?" the Watson Lake gas pumper asked me as he filled my tank.

He had noticed my Alaska license plate. I was not ready to concede that a temperature of fifty below fazed me.

"Yeah, well," I said, "up north it is getting more serious, seventy below when I left Fairbanks."

"That's getting cold," he allowed. "We was near eighty last winter, but didn't shut down."

"I was in Barrow last winter," I countered, "three weeks, never shut my car ignition off. Turn her off to gas up and you got a block of ice."

"Earlier days we had it colder," he said, refusing to give up. "Just didn't expect to have running water all winter."

"Water is always the problem," I said. "I called a plumber the other night in Fairbanks. Not too bright a guy. He detached the pipe from the main intake, put his blowtorch on it. Of course, water gushed in from the main. Ninety minutes before the water company could get out and close the main. Five feet of water in the basement, furnace drowned. Plumber hung in and charged me double because it was Sunday."

I should not have told that true story because it made me look as dumb as the plumber. That's one of the risks of trying to win the cold story contest. I don't know what it is about our competitive natures that turns every cold conversation into a match—maybe it's the cold.

Cold in the North is a fact of life. Disregard the cliché about cold being "a state of mind." The mind has nothing to do with it when the mercury contracts to forty below. Below that, conditions can become perilous to machines and men.

Many have recorded their cold stories in travel annals. Eric Olson described the cold he experienced on a highway trip in January 1982. At Fort St. John the temperature ranged from minus forty to fifty degrees F, but the forecast was for "clear and colder." He was driving a truck that had been winterized in Kansas, and he and his friend had the proper cold-weather clothing, so they pushed on. At Muncho Lake the temperature dropped to minus thirty-eight degrees C and then, during the night, to minus forty-five degrees.

The steering wheel became difficult to turn as the cold froze the grease in the steering box. At Whitehorse the news was that colder temperatures could be expected to the north. It was minus forty, the point at which Celsius and Fahrenheit scales coincide. The men's engine overheated, their tires flattened out, and the defroster could no longer keep the windows from frosting over.

Stopping for gas, Olson did not dare turn off the engine for fear that it would not restart. He should not have set the brakes, either: The brake pads froze to the wheel drums. It took plenty of rocking at full power to unseat the brakes.

Now it was minus sixty C and minus seventy-six F. The record low recorded at Snag, which was not far away, was minus 81.3 F, recorded in 1947. At the border the temperature was minus sixty-two F. At Northway the men got into a heated garage, checked everything, and removed the cardboard radiator shield, which ended their overheating problem. Temperatures remained cold, but they breezed the rest of the way to Fairbanks.

Driving in the cold is one thing; working in it is another. The winter of 1943, when the highway was constructed, was plenty cold for Jerry Hill and the other men who put in a telephone line along the highway from Dawson Creek to Fairbanks. Working at Watson Lake, Hill dug holes for telephone poles with hand equipment, including a seven-foot steel digging bar; a sharpshooter; a shovel with a straight blade;

and a spoon, a shovel with a spoon-shaped blade. It took two hours to dig some holes and all day to dig others, depending upon soil conditions. The job involved pounding the frozen ground with the digging bar until enough dirt was chipped loose to scoop out with the spoon.

"Every day was colder than the one before," Hill recalled. "Few animals were astir in the frozen land. An occasional wolf could be heard howling in the distance, as if protesting his lot in the harsh land. Gas lines froze on many trucks. Wheels froze and wouldn't turn on other trucks. Oil wouldn't pour from a can."

Men suffered, too. Some froze their cheeks just walking fifty yards from the garage to their bunkhouse. Hill froze two fingers while working and, for a time, feared amputation.

Mile 612.9: Watson Lake

Watson Lake is the first Yukon Territory community reached by northbound travelers on the highway. According to James W. Phillips, in *Alaska-Yukon Place Names*, the lake, once called Fish Lake, was renamed for a British Klondike stampeder, Frank Watson. Watson gave up trying to get to the gold field in 1898, settled down as a trapper, and married an Indian woman. He died in 1938. Another story of Watson Lake attributes the name to Bob Watson, who opened a trading post in 1936. Whatever the name origin, the community developed significantly when it was chosen as the site of an airfield on the Northwest staging route and linked to the Alaska Highway in 1942. The log building that was the original airport has been designated a historic building.

The community borders both sides of the highway and has a population of 1,700. Its main industry is forest products.

Bitten by a Seal. Travel can provide unexpected joys in randomly heard conversations. In Edward McCourt's pleasant travel narrative, *Yukon and Northwest Territories* (1969), he tells a charming story of a fleeting encounter in the main street of Watson Lake. Through the dust haze he saw approaching two miniskirted Alaska-bound California girls in the company of a handsome white-haired elderly gentleman wearing a flaming red shirt. As McCourt had seen and exchanged greetings with the girls several times at other road stops when they were alone, he expected more pleasantries in this encounter. But it was not to be. The pretty girls, apparently entranced by their new companion, had no glance for McCourt or anyone else. "All their attention was fixed on the white-haired gentleman. 'And then,' I heard him say as we drew abreast, 'I was bitten by a seal. At thirteen thousand feet.'"

McCourt burned with envy at the splendid raconteur who, like Othello of his Desdemona, could say, "She loved me for the dangers I had passed." And he was furious at not hearing the whole story. Perhaps the man was a fraud and a liar and had not been bitten by a seal at all. McCourt had heard a phrase that had pleased the girls without concerning them, whereas he was certain to lose many nights' sleep wondering about it. "How in God's name could a man be bitten by a seal at thirteen thousand feet?" Alaskans, used to bush pilot tales about the awakening of drugged bears being freighted by air, could have eased McCourt's mind. Such things happen. Seals bite. Not to worry.

But McCourt, a good storyteller himself, wanted to worry—and to have some fun. He concluded his anecdote with a reverie on "the little things. Printed words. Spoken words. And tangible objects which in ordinary circumstances would not arouse the faintest curiosity but in the extraordinary circumstances under which I so often find them in the course of my wanderings serve to oppress me with the awful burden of the unsolved riddles of existence."

Campbell Highway Junction and Sign Forest. The Campbell Highway (Yukon Route 4) leads north to Ross River and Faro. The Sign Forest is prominent here, an imposing array of signposts that have been multiplying since 1942, when an American soldier put up a sign giving the mileage to his hometown. Ever since travelers have been bringing signs for their own towns to create today's colorful forest.

The Alaska Highway Interpretive Center is located at this point as well. If you missed the World War II movie about the highway construction at the Dawson Creek Station Museum, you can see it here, along with other displays on the highway and its construction.

Mile 620: Upper Liard River Bridge

The history of the Liard River country is described in Chapter 5.

Mile 626.2: Cassiar Highway Junction

Travelers diverging on this route to the south go through the Cassiar district, which drew the first gold stampeders north in 1871. The history of the Cassiar region is closely bound to that of the highway because fur traders, prospectors, and other travelers moved back and forth between both regions.

Mile 664.3: Lower Rancheria River Bridge

The Rancheria River was named in the 1870s by American prospectors from California who applied the Mexican term *rancheria*, meaning farm compound, to an Indian settlement on the riverbank. The highway to the north follows the Rancheria River as far as Swift River.

At the Rancheria River I heard one of my favorite highway stories. It took place in the summer of 1954 and illustrates that the road offers a few bumps amid the scenic grandeur. A family from Iowa—wife, husband, two kids—was pushing north in two cars. When they finally reached Dawson Creek, Mrs. Smith was reaching the end of her rope: She was weary of traveling, afraid of the road, and uneasy about the family's prospects in Alaska. And the youngsters were acting out. Who could blame her for being discouraged when the road out of Dawson Creek seemed a rutted, perilous mire likely to engulf her car and children?

Mr. Smith was not too happy, either, having heard a ceaseless round of complaints for hundreds of miles and being worn out from the labors of keeping two cars moving. Although they were just hitting the bad road, he had already repaired eight flats. Mrs. Smith was not the pioneer type. She affected the hair fashion and genteel manners of the Eisenhower era and looked a lot like Pat Nixon, the vice-president's wife. The Smith convoy did not start early in the morning, nor did it go many hours of the day, because Mrs. Smith believed in good grooming for herself and her family.

Anyway, Mrs. Smith looked at the mire and refused to go on. If hubby wanted to go to Alaska, he could drive both cars. She would ride along as a passenger. If he did not like that idea, they could turn around and head for home.

Mr. Smith was resolute, so he drove the 1,500 miles twice, leapfrogging the two cars, catching rides back down the highway once he had moved a car forward thirty miles or so. Drivers going south were glad to give him rides and were well rewarded when he explained his circumstances. Mrs. Smith became a legend on the highway, representing for many everything that was not quite right about the 1950s.

One can only wonder how the Smiths fared when Mrs. Smith faced her first winter in Fairbanks.

Mile 673.4: Hard Driving

The steep grade at this point reminds drivers that the fearsome reputation of the highway has a clear basis. Since construction the stretch between Watson Lake and Teslin has been noted for its steep grades and sharp curves, and it is still feared when the road is icy.

Mile 699.1: Great River Divide

A marker at the turnout notes the divide between rivers that drain into the Arctic Ocean by way of the Mackenzie River and those that drain into the Pacific Ocean by way of the Yukon River.

Mile 702.2: Swift River Bridge

For several decades after the highway construction, Swift River had a station to facilitate transmissions for the communications system and an army installation for road maintenance crews. Repeater stations were placed every 100 miles; Summit Lake and Muncho Lake were other sites. The stations also had schools serving the children of families living there. The Swift River buildings have been moved or destroyed.

Visiting Swift River in 1989, Norm Drayton, a former supervisor for the telephone and telegraph service, was amazed that the place had not survived. He and his wife had raised their children at Swift River, Muncho Lake, Summit Lake, and Whitehorse in the 1950s and recalled their life on the highway with fondness. Like many northerners, they moved outside after retirement, in 1972, but only because of higher living costs.

Drayton drove the highway constantly on his job and had many narrow escapes ("I never told Beth about these when I got back home") on the road. Winter conditions were often so dangerous that even in emergencies "I did not dare touch the brakes." Ice was the chief hazard, and chains did not help. The only time Drayton used them over a bad stretch he lost control and slid off the road. Near mining areas speeding ore trucks crowding the road were also frightening. Drivers needed daring to pass on narrow sections, and some truckers had plenty.

Despite the hazards, Drayton found the driving pleasurable in most seasons, partly because of the abundance of wildlife that could be observed. When the rabbit population was high, a driver could not avoid crunching them on the road. "Those years there was lots of food for wolves."

Drayton also enjoyed fishing along the highway: "It was fantastic." The Draytons lived at Historic Mile 733, and the river at Historic 739 offered a wonderful fishing hole. "An old tree jutted across the stream at that point," Drayton said. "I could look down on the fish from there. They were everywhere." He was delighted to find the same conditions on his 1989 trip.

For all his nostalgia for earlier days, Drayton found the highway country even more beautiful on his recent journey because road improvements have provided better views.

Mile 710.5: British Columbia Boundary Crossing

The highway crosses into British Columbia for a stretch of 42 miles.

Mile 735.8: Smart River Bridge

The original name was Smartz River, after a local Indian family. Error or laziness changed it to Smart River.

Mile 752.3: Morley River Bridge

The Morley River, which flows into Teslin Lake, was named for W. Morley Ogilvie, an assistant to Arthur St. Cyr on the 1897 survey of the Telegraph Creek–Teslin Lake route.

Mile 757.9: Monument to Soldier Builder

A marker here commemorates a soldier who died during the highway construction. It reads: "In memory of Max Richardson 39163467, Corporal Co F 340th Eng. Army of the United States; born October 10, 1918; died October 17, 1942. Faith is the victory."

Mile 776: Nisutlin Bay Bridge

Nisutlin is an Indian word for "quiet waters." Construction of the Nisutlin Bay Bridge at Teslin Lake taxed the ingenuity of the engineers during the time of highway construction because the bay is so deep. Timber structures could not penetrate 247 feet of muck, as modern steel structures can; the builders made do with a support that held up for several years.

The original structure was 2,300 feet long, the longest trestle on the highway. The longest trestle poles were 180 feet, not long enough to penetrate the foundation of mud. Canadian engineer James Quong believed that the foundation would have been too shaky but for the stringers that helped pin the bridge to the shores: "The whole length of it was so pinned together that it was like a string of beads, so that the bridge was really a string from one side to another. You'd look along the centerline; you'd see it bow to one side and then back again." Before the structure was replaced, Quong used to fear the breakup and the huge blocks of ice, "like battleships," that would come roaring downriver at the bridge. "When [the ice] hits that bridge, you know, she really leans over to one side. And we used to spend many, many winters just repairing the piles that were bashed up by the ice."

Today's drivers have a good view of the lake and Teslin village from the bridge. Teslin is a corruption of the Indian word *Teslintoo* for "long narrow waters," and the lake *is* long—86 miles. It forms part of the British Columbia–Yukon Territory boundary.

Mile 776.3: Teslin

The Indian village of Teslin developed around a trading post established in 1903. Present population is 450.

George Johnson. The George Johnson Museum, which displays exhibits on local history, including the gold rush and Tlingit Indian culture, is named for a Teslin Tlingit (1884–1972) whose photographs capture people and events of Atlin and Teslin between 1910 and 1940. A trapper, Johnson was also a hunting guide even though a government regulation of 1923 denied Indians the right to be guides except as assistants to white men. Later this regulation was changed to give government officials discretion in determining which Indians were qualified to handle the paperwork required of chief guides.

Johnson operated the first taxi service in the area, using a 1928 Chevrolet on a three-mile summer road he built several years before the Alaska Highway was constructed. During the winter he offered more extensive transport service: He drove on the ice of Lake Teslin.

A post of the Royal North-West Mounted Police (as the Mounties were renamed in 1904) was established at Teslin in 1904. The police tried to restrict the flow of liquor to the Indians from British Columbia and Alaska, but Indians were free to cross into Alaska to buy liquor, and the Mounties' restrictions were ineffective.

During the winter of 1942–43, while the highway was under construction, the community suffered from successive attacks of measles, influenza, mumps, dysentery, whooping cough, jaundice, and meningitis. Many Indians died.

Mile 803: View of Yukon Lakes

For many miles travelers have the Yukon lakes within view. The highway runs along Lake Teslin for thirty miles from about Mile 803. Its waters are beautiful and peaceful, offering no reminder of desperate Klondike stampeders who traveled up the Stikine River from the coast at Wrangell to reach the head of navigation at Telegraph Creek. From Telegraph Creek, named for the abortive Western Union Telegraph construction project of 1865–67, stampeders pushed overland to Teslin, built boats on the lake, then followed the Teslin River to the Yukon River fifty miles below Whitehorse.

Mile 808.2: Canol Road Junction

Junction here with the Canol Road (Yukon Highway 6). The Canol Road was abandoned in 1945 and rebuilt and opened to summer traffic in 1958. The 136.8-mile section from the Alaska Highway to Ross River on the Campbell Highway is called the South Canol Road. It receives minimum maintenance along its narrow, twisted, scenic course.

Black Gold. The Canol Road was built in 1942–44 by U.S. army engineers to support a petroleum pipeline from an oil field at Norman Wells in the Northwest Territories. It was hoped that the petroleum from Norman Wells could be used to fuel airplanes on the Northwest staging route and trucks along the Alaska Highway. This $134 million project cost as much as the Alaska Highway and was almost as difficult an engineering venture.

Canol was an ill-conceived defense project that did not achieve the expectations of its planners. Production from Norman Wells was limited, and transport over the line was beset with difficulties. Furthermore, as it turned out, the Japanese did not disrupt North Pacific shipping routes, so there was no real need of an alternative source of petroleum in the North. The operation was closed down in 1945.

Republican members of the U.S. Congress investigated the costs and limited production of the facility in an effort to embarrass President Harry Truman. Truman's critics called Canol "a colossal blunder" and "fiasco," which was true, but the detractors overlooked the anxieties of military planners in 1942. When Canol and the Alaska Highway were proposed in 1942, the U.S. Navy had not yet won any battles with the Japanese navy, and a successful invasion of Alaska by Japanese forces seemed probable. At the same time German U-boats in the Atlantic and Caribbean were sinking tankers at will. American officials feared that Alaska's defense would be impossible if supplies of oil from California were disrupted and no other sources were available.

The extent of the oil field reserves at Norman Wells, 400 miles northwest of Whitehorse, was not known, but it was the only identified field in the region. The army engineers started work at Norman Wells and on the pipeline in the spring of 1942. Planners hoped that oil would flow in five months, but it took a force of 4,000 soldiers and 12,000 civilian workers two years before the first barrel of oil was produced.

Canol demonstrated that the planners had not given enough consideration to the travails and costs involved in developing an unproven oil field near the Arctic Circle and conveying its product hundreds of miles by pipeline. The army spent $17 million prospecting and developing wells; $27 million on transportation and road construction; $31 million to lay a 550-mile-long, four-inch-diameter pipeline along the ground between Norman Wells and Whitehorse; and $24 million for the purchase of a Corpus Christi refinery that was dismantled and shipped by rail and steamship to Skagway, then by rail to Whitehorse for assembly. In magnitude, the project bore some resemblance to that carried out decades later to bring Prudhoe Bay oil across Alaska to Valdez by pipeline—a successful but costly project that benefited from modern advances in transport technology.

Norman Wells's oil holds the record for the most expensive ever produced. At a time when oil was selling for $1 a barrel, the United States paid $100 million for one million barrels of oil—or $100 a barrel. Yet Canol was not a total loss. Engineers constructed a $35 million gasoline storage and pipeline system, which included a feeder line from Skagway to Whitehorse, and a 900-mile-long pipeline paralleling the Alaska Highway between Watson Lake and Fairbanks. Gasoline shipped by tanker from California to Skagway was sent over the new pipeline to the interior and used by the army for trucks carrying freight on the Alaska Highway.

Mile 808.6: Teslin River Bridge

Before the construction of the highway, freight was carried between Teslin and Whitehorse on the Teslin River. When the highway was completed, the British Yukon Navigation Company halted its steamboat service.

Mile 808.9: Johnson's Crossing

George Johnson, the Teslin Indian photographer (see Mile 776.3), operated a ferry across the Teslin River at this point during the highway construction days. But James W. Phillips, *Alaska-Yukon Place Names*, finds the origin of the placename in a U.S. Army engineer named Johnson who designated the crossing site. The George Johnson origin seems more likely.

The Hitchhiker. It was at Johnson's Crossing that I heard the hitchhiker story. My informant had been driving south and had stopped at Johnson's Crossing for a portly, middle-aged fellow who was holding both thumbs out, pointing in either direction. The discouraged-looking hitchhiker was standing beside an old, beat-up Ford with flat tires.

"South or north?" asked the driver.

"Which way you going?" the hitchhiker asked warily.

"South."

He reflected a moment, seemed indecisive, and finally explained. George and his wife, Bonnie Mae, Texans, were heading for Fairbanks and a possible job for him on the North Slope. As each was driving a car, they could be together only at pit stops, meals, and in the evening. But they got into a long-running quarrel early in the trip. George refused to believe that Billy Sol Estes and some other Texas crooks had really been touched with grace and become genuine born-again Christians. Too many fellows, most of them behind bars or otherwise in hot water, had been getting born-again—and he was suspicious. Well, his wife figured he might just as well ask for immediate admission to hell, since he was certain to go there anyway for doubting sudden conversions. Bonnie Mae cried and raged one whole day over his damnation, then was silent the entire next day. The silence worried him, and he kept his wallet and car keys hidden under his pillow at night. But he woke to find that Bonnie Mae had gone. Outside he discovered that someone had punched in all four of his tires with a sharp instrument and used lipstick to scribble graffiti on his windshield, mostly references to Scriptures: "Read John 23, you ass," and other endearments.

Religion can be a powerful divider. George was glum, the old car was not worth the cost of new tires, and he was indecisive about continuing north or following Bonnie Mae south. Might his destiny be to the north? Maybe someone was showing him a sign. When last seen he stood beside the road with his thumb firmly pointed in that direction.

Mile 836.8: Jake's Corner

The road to Atlin, Yukon Highway 7, branches here. Atlin, fifty-seven miles south, is a uniquely attractive gold rush town on the shore of a great lake. The road was built in 1949 by Canadian army engineers. Atlin developed from gold discoveries made in July 1898.

According to James W. Phillips, in *Alaska-Yukon Place Names*, the crossing (which also provides access to Carcross) was either named for U.S. Army engineer Captain Jacobson or a Teslin Indian, Jake Jackson, who often camped in the area on treks to Carcross.

Mile 852.7: Marsh Lake

Marsh Lake is part of the Yukon River headwaters and was named by Lt. Frederick Schwatka for Professor O. C. Marsh of Yale University. Marsh was famed as a paleontologist and ornithologist. From 1883–96 he was president of the National Academy of Scientists.

Schwatka's Voyage. Pivotal events in the Yukon and Alaska's mining history were the discovery of gold at Juneau in 1880 and the efforts of the U.S. Army to develop the interior route from Lynn Canal. Lt. Frederick Schwatka led an expedition in 1883 to chart the Yukon River from its source to its mouth. While the Yukon was hardly unknown, the army aimed to fix its course precisely. Everywhere in the West the waterways had been a primary part of the transportation network, and the Yukon's 2,300-mile length made it appear to be a main artery. The initial penetration route had been from its mouth at Norton Sound, but entry from its source, much closer to Juneau and the Pacific Coast ports, made sense.

When Schwatka landed near the mouth of the Chilkat River, he hired Chilkat Indians to pack his baggage. After Schwatka got over the pass, he built a raft on Lake Lindeman for his Yukon voyage. On the upper Yukon he met two "woe-begone" prospectors, dropouts from a prospecting party of that season who were returning to the coast. Along the way Schwatka met other prospectors who were faring somewhat better, including Joe Ladue, later to be a founding father of Dawson. Ladue and Schwatka met amidst the watery maze of the Yukon Flats, where the soldiers suffered three weeks of confusion working their raft downriver. At Nuklukayet, near the Tanana, Schwatka abandoned his raft in favor of Arthur Harper's steamer and voyaged down to St. Michael in more comfort.

Schwatka's voyage was not one of discovery, as Russian, British, and American traders and prospectors had preceded him. But Schwatka compiled a good chart that was used by many voyagers during the Klondike rush. His popular voyage narrative, *Along Alaska's Great River*, made its many American readers more aware of the newly acquired territory and its potential. Some Canadians were annoyed that Schwatka freely named places in Canada, but that is the prerogative of explorers regardless of nationality.

George Dawson's 1887 Survey. Geologist George Dawson, for whom Dawson Creek and Dawson City are named, made the first Canadian government survey of this region in 1887. His survey brought him into Alaska Highway country at the lakes, and he continued near it for much of his journey. Starting from Wrangell, he ascended the Stikine River, moved into the interior to Frances Lake and its drainage system, then reached the upper Yukon River. At Dyea he was pleased to report on the completion of "our fourth month of arduous and incessant travel . . . by rivers, lakes, and portages of the interior . . . the total distance traversed being about 1322 miles."

In official reports Dawson did not often show any exuberance over natural scenery, but he was impressed by Marsh Lake and the Yukon headwater country: "It is a singularly picturesque region, abounding in striking points of view and in landscapes pleasing in their variety, or grand and impressive in their combination of rugged mountain forms."

During the 1897–98 Klondike gold rush, stampeders, who crossed either the Chilkoot Pass from Dyea or the White Pass from Skagway, built boats and followed the chain of lakes, including Marsh Lake, to White Horse Rapids and on to Dawson City.

Mile 854.4: Highway Construction Camp

In 1942 on this site, Historical Mile 883, the Marsh Lake Construction Camp housed army road builders. For the fortieth anniversary of the highway in 1982 historical plaques marking the former camps were erected at all campsites.

Mile 861.1: M'Clintock River

The M'Clintock River was named for Francis M'Clintock by Frederick Schwatka. Schwatka had made an arctic expedition several years before his Yukon voyage and was interested in other polar explorers, including M'Clintock. Schwatka honored him for several polar expeditions, particularly that of 1857–59, when he traced the movements of explorer John Franklin's expedition.

Mile 874.4: Klondike Highway Junction

Just as it had been during the Klondike gold rush, Skagway became the hub of transportation, communication, and supply for highway builders. In the fall of 1942 the army built new dock and cargo handling facilities at Skagway in anticipation of the heavy demands of highway construction. At that time the highway construction corridor could not be reached by road from Skagway, but the White Pass & Yukon Railway, completed in 1900, was available for service to the interior as far as Whitehorse. With the approval of the Canadian government, the U.S. Army leased the railroad for the duration of the war and shipped much of the construction equipment and materials to Carcross. From Carcross army engineers built a road to Historical Mile 905 (Mile 874.4). Whitehorse was the other destination for construction personnel and material.

The army replaced the White Pass railway's ancient rolling stock with twenty-four new locomotives and 284 freight cars. Because traffic had been light for a number of years as mining production declined, the railroad had been getting by with inferior equipment. During the 1930s the train sometimes ran only once a week during the winter, and it shut down entirely if snowfalls were heavy. Army engineers determined that the roadbed could handle wartime freight needs and give it a complete rehabilitation. With the upgraded roadbed and rolling stock the railroad was able to move as many as 23 trains daily during the summer of 1943.

Because good communication among Skagway, Whitehorse, and highway points was deemed essential, the army modernized the system. Army engineers laid a new telephone and telegraph line from Skagway to Whitehorse that tied in with a new line built along the route of the Alaska Highway between Edmonton and Fairbanks. This communication line, called Catel for Canadian Telephone, was an extensive network that used 14,000 miles of wire and 95,000 poles. It gave Alaska and northwestern Canada an effective communications system that was not affected by the radio blackouts that had plagued the old system.

Klondike Highway 2, opened in 1978 between Carcross and Skagway, allowed road travelers direct access to the historic gold rush town and its port for the first time.

This junction will interest travelers who wish to trace either the highway construction history or that of the Klondike stampeders to their starting points at Skagway and Dyea. Most of the stampeders who did not voyage up the Yukon River from its mouth at St. Michael traveled over the Chilkoot or White passes from Dyea or Skagway.

Mile 867.3: Yukon River Bridge

At this point travelers can see the upper Yukon River. The dam was built by the British Yukon Navigation Company in 1923 to facilitate steamboat traffic. Before, during periods of low water in the spring, boats were sometimes unable to operate. The facility and its additions are now maintained by the Northern Canada Power Commission.

The Yukon River flows 1,980 miles from here to reach the Bering Sea, sweeping in a wide arc across the northern Yukon Territory and Alaska. The Yukon's main branch is the Pelly River, originating in the Mackenzie Range of the eastern Rockies. About 150 miles south of Whitehorse the Pelly River joins the Yukon branch (called the Lewes River until 1952), which started from lakes on the eastern side of the Coast Range. The Yukon River originates in Lake Marsh and other nearby lakes and is one of the world's longest.

Except for the upper stretch near Whitehorse, the long river is untrammeled by dams on its passage to the Bering Sea. With its tributaries it provided access to the interior of Alaska and the Yukon Territory last century and, for a time, floated puffing wood- and oil-burning steamboats hauling passengers and freight. With the development of roads and railroads the river reverted to wilderness state. Today you may voyage by small boat, stopping if you wish at the several small communities along the way. One recent book of such a voyage that makes pleasant reading is *Reading the River: A Voyage Down the Yukon*, by John Hildebrand.

Mile 876.8: Wolf Creek Bridge

This bridge was washed out by flooding in 1949. Canadian army men quickly replaced it and then were embarrassed to discover that the structure would support only unloaded trucks. After another, better-supervised job, the new bridge proved able to handle traffic.

Mile 879.6: Point of Interest: 135th meridian

A sign at this point indicates that the highway is near the 135th meridian.

Mile 880.4: Whitehorse Copper Mines

A turnoff here goes to the Whitehorse Copper Mines, which is no longer operating. Mining in the Whitehorse copper belt revived in the early 1970s, continuing for some years until low copper prices made mining unprofitable. The Whitehorse Copper Mines closed in 1981.

Mile 884: Miles Canyon and Schwatka Lake Access

This is the turnoff for the South Access Road to Whitehorse and for access to the hydroelectric dam, Miles Canyon, and Schwatka Lake.

Whitehorse and the Klondike Gold Rush

It's a hard old life,
but if we strike it rich,
all is well.
— *George Hazelet*

The faith of the northern prospectors in the mineral resources of Alaska rested on the history of western mining. Gold discoveries in California in 1848 caused a stampede of thousands to the Pacific Coast. Subsequently prospectors found gold in Arizona, Nevada, Idaho, Montana, the Dakotas, and elsewhere. Inevitably men turned northward to search for wealth and found rewards on the Fraser River in 1858 and the Caribou a year later.

In the early 1870s the Cassiar district of British Columbia as well as Sitka, where the Stewart mine was discovered in 1872, created the excitement. In 1880 major strikes were made at Juneau. As Juneau developed into a thriving community it became the natural jumping-off place to Alaska's interior for most of the prospectors who ventured forth in the 1880s.

The placer deposits of the Cassiar were exhausted by 1884, and most of the miners left the district. Potentially rich auriferous quartz veins could not be mined because of the high costs of importing machinery. Thus Cassiar miners looked north. Why not try the Yukon country, they reflected? Miners knew about explorer Frederick Schwatka and prospectors who had used the Chilkoot Pass into the interior. Ordi-

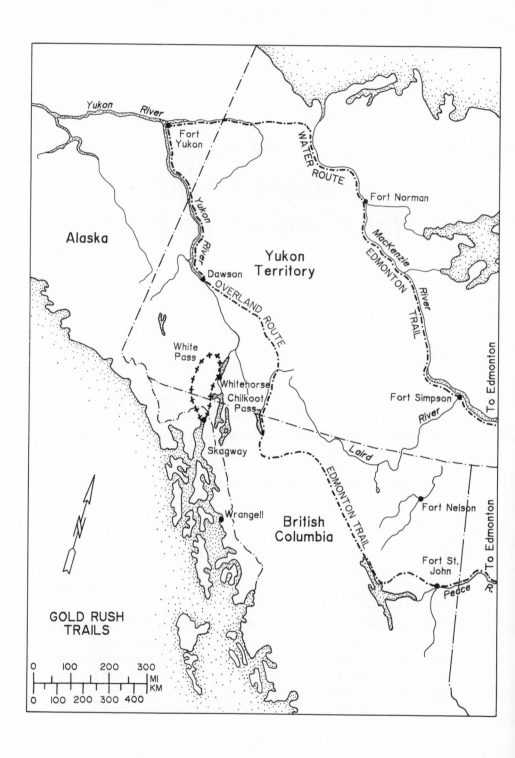

Yukon River

Fort
Yukon

WATER ROUTE

Alaska

Fort Norman

Yukon
River

Yukon
Territory

Dawson

OVERLAND ROUTE

Mackenzie River

EDMONTON TRAIL

To Edmonton

White
Pass

Whitehorse

Chilkoot
Pass

Fort Simpson

River

Skagway

Laird
River

EDMONTON TRAIL

Wrangell

British
Columbia

Fort Nelson

To Edmonton

Fort St.
John

Peace R.

GOLD RUSH
TRAILS

0   100   200   300
                                MI
                                KM
0   100 200 300 400

nary miners lacked the capital for steamer transport on the Yukon, but pushing downriver from the headwaters seemed easy enough.

Some 200 prospectors crossed the Chilkoot in 1883. Reports of successes reached Juneau in 1883–84, although they were probably exaggerated. One messenger spoke of placers yielding $150 a day, another of gravel bars mined for $25 a day. Although most of the prospectors reached the Yukon's tributaries, a few tried other regions, including the Copper River. In the fall of 1883 a miner electrified Juneau by appearing with $1,000 in coarse Yukon gold, stimulating the movement of 300 men into the interior in the spring of 1884.

The interior miners attempted to regulate mining districts and keep order through miners' meetings. Their ability to provide the rudiments of governance was on a par with their ability to extract gold— crude and inefficient but effective for the transitional period. It was probably in 1882 that the first formal miners' meeting convened on the Yukon at Fort Reliance. Mining regulations and the necessity of recordkeeping were of chief concern: "There was a meeting called to make laws governing the size of placer claims and water rights," Jack McQuesten explained, "so that everyone knew what he was entitled to in case anything was struck and then was bounded off and I was elected recorder."

Sitka, the old capital of Russian America, was the scene of the first gold mining in Alaska with the development of the Stewart mine in 1872. Juneau was founded in 1881. Juneau proved to be an important mining center and eventually replaced Sitka as territorial capital. Richard T. Harris and Joseph Juneau made placer and quartz discoveries in 1880 with backing from George E. Pilz, who was building a stamp mill at the Stewart mine, and from other Sitka men.

Juneau's prosperity was assured by the mines and by its location on Lynn Canal, just 100 miles south of the trail leading to the Chilkoot Pass.

Strike at Fortymile

In the mid-1880s prospectors of the interior made their first major gold discovery. The Fortymile River's headwaters lie within Canada, but the river's southerly course crosses the Alaska border before arcing northward again to flow back to Canada. Such a wayward passage resulted in some confusion after the gold discovery, as most of the diggings at Bonanza Bar, Franklin, Chicken, Jack Wade, and Steel

Creek lay within Alaska, whereas the community was within the Yukon region of Canada.

The news of the gold strike reached the coast in dramatic fashion— two Fortymile men made a winter journey that almost took their lives. Anticipating an influx of miners, traders Jack McQuesten and Arthur Harper prepared to move their store from Fort Nelson on the Stewart River to the Fortymile mouth.

The Alaska Commercial Company had maintained a virtual monopoly on interior trade from 1870 until the North American Transportation and Trading Company challenged its dominance in 1892. With the little steamboats *Yukon, St. Michael,* and *New Racket* the ACC serviced its several trading posts efficiently. After the Fortymile development, the company prepared for increased trade by launching the *Arctic,* a larger 140-ton vessel, in 1889. But the new company put 200-ton steamboats modeled on those navigating the Missouri River on the Yukon, and the ACC answered the competition with new, larger boats of its own. In 1898, the ACC put three huge, 700-ton-capacity vessels into service, the *Susie,* the *Sarah,* and the *Hannah.*

Gold was discovered near Circle on Birch Creek, a Yukon tributary within Alaska, in 1892. Other discoveries were made in 1893. The new Alaskan gold field soon proved itself. Although the yield in 1893–94 was only $9,000, the production from the entire Birch Creek district by the end of 1895 was $150,000.

Circle's growth was encouraged by Jack McQuesten, whose store extended credit to at least eighty Fortymile miners. The population reached 700 in 1896, a sizable community for Alaska. Circle's decline followed hard on its peak in 1896 but was not caused by the exhaustion of local mines, as is usual in placer mining districts. The exodus from Circle in 1896–97 began with the stirring news of George Carmack's gold discovery on the Klondike—a development that marked a watershed in northern history.

Carmack's Discovery

George Carmack took the advice of a friend, Robert Henderson, and went prospecting with two Indians, Skookum Jim and Tagish Charlie, along the Klondike, a tributary of the Yukon. Henderson, for reasons he had good cause to regret, did not stake any claims himself and left the region before his friends struck gold on August 17, 1896. Some weeks later, Carmack showed some of his nuggets at Fortymile, and miners dashed to the new bonanza. It took longer for the word to reach Circle, but when it did, most of the population rushed to the Klondike.

Because the Mounties moved quickly from Fortymile, where they had established a post in 1894, to Dawson City, the orderly development of the Klondike was assured. It was the availability of a well-organized, fully empowered national police force that distinguished the Klondike from other western American and Alaskan mining frontiers. Law and order were imposed at once – and stayed imposed; life and property were secure throughout the Canadian North.

In July 1897 the outside world gained its news of the Klondike riches when two ships, *Excelsior* and *Portland,* reached San Francisco and Seattle with rich miners from Dawson City. By July 17, only two days after the *Excelsior* brought the news, San Franciscans were already on the move: "Working men quit their jobs and joined the procession for the long and tedious journey northward," proclaimed the *Chronicle.* When the *Portland* arrived in Seattle with rich miners a day after the *Excelsior* the excitement was even more intense, turning the Puget Sound town "upside down" with a "delirium" of gold fever: "Policemen are resigning from the force, every street car man that can raise a stake has given notice to the company . . . Men neglect their businesses and congregate in groups on the street in excited discussion."

Stampeder Routes to the Klondike

To tell the gold rush story, we must expand our geographic range along the Alaska Highway to consider the various routes to the Klondike. Much of the color and excitement of the mass adventure concerned the stampeder's journey to the North; it was often the most taxing part of the experience. To men and women planning their journey in Seattle, Chicago, or Montreal the routes were well defined. Newspaper stories and guidebooks provided details, giving the costs, distances, and travel times involved. Stampeders made their choices on the basis of this information as well as on the state of their finances, the extent of their baggage, and their judgment of the region most likely to fulfill their golden dreams.

The shortest route to Dawson appeared to be the Chilkoot Pass out of Dyea or the White Pass out of Skagway. Another possibility existed with Jack Dalton's trail from Pyramid Harbor, a route suitable for pack animals, although tolls were levied on passage. Voyaging to St.

Michael and thence up the Yukon by river steamboat appeared to many to be the safest and least arduous of the available routes. Other routes held patriotic appeal, as with the "All-Canadian" overland routes promoted by the Canadian government.

Most stampeders preferred the Chilkoot. Other gates to the interior lacked the drama of the Chilkoot, a mass that was obviously nature's barrier, a rocky challenge to human stamina. In essence the Chilkoot could encapsulate all the real hardships miners had to endure and, in part at least, lend meaning to the undertaking.

The summit of the Chilkoot at 3,100 feet was 20 miles from tidewater. By 1897 a rough trail from tidewater to the base of a steep 500-foot rise to the summit had long since been established. After packers reached the summit the hard part was over. The trail descended gradually seven miles to the lake, which was 1,000 lower in elevation.

The 1897 Klondike stampeders landed at either Dyea or Skagway to begin their trek to the gold field. Through 1897–98 some 30,000 to 40,000 stampeders landed at the head of Lynn Canal after completing their ocean voyages. No brief summary could do justice to the wide diversity of their experiences from the time of landing to their arrival at Dawson or elsewhere. But the records reveal the emotions of the event—anxieties, expectations, frustrations, angers, fears—as well as the physical hardships involved.

Travelers had good reason to feel triumphant in achieving the summit without succumbing to fatigue, discouragement, accident, or avalanche, as most made the trip repeatedly to bring forward their baggage. They moved as part of a disorganized mass, subject to anxiety-producing rumors and fear of the unknown. Emotions weighed as heavily as backpacks in the highly charged atmosphere of the trail.

The Mounties established a customs station at Tagish Lake and another post at the summit to collect fees and turn back travelers lacking 1,000 pounds of food. The food requirement was taken seriously because of the general belief in Dawson in the fall of 1897 that a famine could occur over the winter. Stampeders saw merit in the Mounties' strictness, and those who had worried about the security of lives and property in Skagway and Dyea found their presence reassuring.

Beyond the summit, the next great general activity was boat building at Lake Lindeman for Chilkoot stampeders or at Lake Bennett for White Pass travelers. There was plenty of time for boat building for winter or spring arrivals because they had to wait for the the thaw of the Yukon's headwaters before pushing on.

The Yukon River passage cost a number of lives. Many stampeders were inexperienced as boatmen, and a number of rapids, including the terrible White Horse, had to be traversed or portaged. Finally, the Mounties began supervision of navigation, requiring women and children to walk around the White Horse and prohibiting boats built without adequate freeboard. These restrictions probably saved some lives.

How long did it take to reach the Klondike? The journey's duration varied widely depending on the season. Travelers who reached the lakes while navigation was possible could ready boats within a week or two and be under way. In about a week they could pass the dangerous part of the river—if they had no accidents—and reach Lake Laberge and a safe, easy drift of 400 miles to Dawson, which took approximately a week to ten days.

Other Routes to the Gold Field

Rushers who did not enter the country from Lynn Canal or the mouth of the Yukon River used one of the several Canadian overland routes. The Canadian routes caused considerable grief to argonauts, and these trails, particularly that from Edmonton, have been discussed in Chapter 3.

The Ashcroft Trail from Ashcroft, B.C., 125 miles northeast of Vancouver, was another touted Canadian route. Travelers took the Caribou Road, built in the 1860s during the Caribou gold rush, crossed Sheena River, and after 1,000 miles reached the Stikine at Telegraph Creek. The route seemed to offer certain benefits: lower transportation costs, the Caribou trail, and the trail constructed by the Western Union Telegraph Expedition in the mid-1800s, but the advantages were illusory, since the trails were hardly more than a trace. Of the approximately 1,500 men who attempted the route because of its so-called "easy" access with pack animals, the greater number turned back after their animals died. It was said that none of the few travelers who reached Dawson had pack animals on arrival.

The Yukon Route

For stampeders who considered an all-water route to Klondike preferable to packing over the Chilkoot or White passes, the Yukon entry was well advertised by shipping companies. It was the more expensive route but was certainly safer and less arduous. From Seattle to St. Michael the ocean voyage was 2,750 miles. The voyage could be comfortable or miserable depending upon the time it took, the weather, the quality of the ship, and—most important—the number of passengers. Some shipping companies took gross advantage of the desperation of the Klondike-bound travelers and crammed them aboard without regard for comfort. Postponement of sailing dates was an aggravation, as were delays caused by engine malfunction, storms, or ice on the Bering Sea.

Most ships called at Dutch Harbor in the Aleutians for refueling or other purposes. At St. Michael, a dismal spot, passengers transferred to one of the steamboats serving the Yukon. Over 1897–98 the Yukon fleet grew mightily as trading companies, shipping companies, and individuals anticipated a bonanza in freight and passenger fares. But it was some 1,700 miles upriver to Dawson, and few of the 1897 stampeders were quick enough off the mark to reach St. Michael before freeze-up. Some of them returned to the states, others languished at St. Michael, and a few pushed overland.

For the Yukon voyage, passenger accommodations were either on the steamboat itself or on a barge that larger boats pushed ahead. A barge could carry up to 175 people in crude fashion, with rows of berths lining its sides and separated by a long dining table running the length of the vessel. There was no protection from mosquitoes or from the tedium of the lower river landscape, and anxieties mounted when the vessels grounded on sandbars. Sometimes passengers endured major delays that were particularly aggravating in late season.

In the fall everyone aboard scanned the skies apprehensively for weather signs and viewed the first ice with sinking hearts. Usually progress was steady, if slow; the boats pushed against a four-to-five-mile current and made about six miles an hour. Halts to take on wood were about two hours daily in the commercial boats but much longer for independents, who did their own woodcutting. Steamboat fare was expensive because of high costs, and one important cost factor was the price of wood—varying from $7 a cord downriver to $14 nearer Dawson. A large steamboat driving a barge needed thirty cords a day.

Stops at towns provided some diversion. At places like Rampart, Forty Mile, Fort Yukon, and Circle some passengers met acquaintances from outside and could enjoy gossip and opinions on the country that might be more trustworthy than those gathered from strangers. Some passengers ended their voyage at ports like Rampart, either because mining prospects seemed better than those at Dawson or when ice stopped navigation.

Mile 884: Whitehorse

Driving north on the Alaska Highway travelers follow the Yukon River and the tracks of the White Pass & Yukon Railway past Miles Canyon, Schwatka Lake, and a hydroelectric dam.

Whitehorse is the capital of the Yukon Territory and its administrative, transportation, and supply center. Its population is 20,000, which is more than two thirds of the entire population of the territory.

The town was born during the 1897–98 gold rush as a rest stop for stampeders who ran their boats through the Whitehorse Rapids, the last great river obstacle faced by those who climbed the passes from Lynn Canal. The dreaded rapids have disappeared since the construction of a hydroelectric dam and the creation of Schwatka Lake, named for the army explorer Frederick Schwatka, who charted the Yukon River in 1883.

In its impact upon development the gold rush was the biggest thing that ever happened in northern British Columbia, the Yukon, and Alaska. But for the discovery and long-term production of minerals, we would not have had the early development of permanent settlements in much of the North.

White Pass and Yukon Railway. Whitehorse's permanence was assured in 1900 when it became the terminus for the White Pass and Yukon Railway operating from tidewater at Skagway. As Dawson City was 300 miles downriver, Whitehorse remained an important steamboat terminus as well. Summer travelers between Whitehorse and Dawson moved from train to riverboat, while winter travelers reached and left Whitehorse over surface trails over which established stage outfits ran horse sleds.

The railroad built shipyards at Whitehorse and Dawson and branched into Yukon River navigation with its subsidiary, the British Yukon Navigation Company. Other steamboat lines could not match the convenience passengers and shippers gained from the rail connection, and by 1904 most of those on the upper Yukon had given up. By 1910 the railroad company's boats dominated the lower Yukon as well, and most of Whitehorse's residents were employed by the railroad or its subsidiaries. By charging high freight rates the company pleased its stockholders, but the rates hurt marginal mining and other businesses. The economy languished, and the company's profits also fell.

Historically, the town and region depended almost entirely upon mining for its prosperity. As mining declined so did Whitehorse. In the 1930s the population was around 300 in winter, although it might soar to 1,000 in the summer.

The highway construction in 1942 boosted Whitehorse. Thanks to the highway, Whitehorse became the territorial capital in 1953. Dawson City, which had been bypassed, declined further while the new capital gained residents and benefited from an extensive building program.

Canadians were not always happy with the American military presence in Whitehorse. The engineers sometimes seemed pushy and inconsiderate of their hosts, but wholehearted cooperation in the highway construction overwhelmed resentment. It is worth noting that in Skagway, at least, the Americans complained more bitterly than the Canadians about the high-handedness of the U.S. military.

Regional gold, zinc, and copper mining revived in the 1960s and 1970s to give a bloom to the Whitehorse and Yukon economy. Low prices in the 1980s forced the closure of copper mines, but gold mining has been lively for several years. With the stability of government payrolls, Whitehorse is less affected by the boom-or-bust mining cycle than in former times, but the mineral industry will determine future growth.

The White Pass & Yukon Railway did not carry many passengers in post–World War II years except for tourists in the summer, but it made good profits for many years hauling ore to the coast for shipment outside. The railroad reduced service in the late 1970s, then quit operation after the Skagway-Whitehorse Highway opened in 1978. Excursion rail service for tourists from Skagway over the White Pass started again in 1987, but the trains do not get beyond the lake country. Travelers who want to take the historic railroad from Whitehorse can get a bus in summer to reach the train.

Historic Attractions: McBride Museum. The McBride Museum, located downtown, has one of the finest collections of material on the Klondike gold rush that can be found. It also has riverboat exhibits and exhibits on other phases of Yukon history and wildlife.

The Sam McGee Cabin in the McBride Museum and the Robert Service Campground at Mile 884 will stimulate visitors who are fans of the Bard of the Yukon.

Robert Service. Robert Service's poems are so closely identified with the Klondike gold rush that it is a shock to discover he did not experience it. He was born in Scotland and emigrated to North America in 1902. While living in California he became enthralled with the North, primarily through reading the stories of Jack London. The Klondike still retained its magic in the early years of this century, even though Nome and Fairbanks had replaced Dawson as the vibrant mining centers. Service read about the Malamute Kid and other London characters and dreamed about the wonderful land of adventure. He did not imagine that "while other men were seeking Eldorado, they were also making one for me."

His opportunity to find Eldorado came by chance. In 1904, he was offered a bank clerk's job at the Whitehorse branch of a Canadian bank. Service moved north happily to enjoy the country he had read so much about. He lived sedately in Whitehorse but enjoyed reciting famous verses like "Casey at the Bat" and "The Face on the Bar-Room Floor" at social gatherings. After one such performance Stroller White, the well-known *Whitehorse Star* journalist, urged him to write original verse: "Give us something about our own little bit of earth . . ., There's a rich paystreak waiting for someone to work. Why don't you go on in and stake it?"

Service thought about White's suggestion for some time before inspiration came. He described the moment in his autobiography. It was Saturday night, and he was still working at the bank. Music and revelry from a neighboring saloon penetrated his reflections. Just then a pistol shot roared in his ear, fired by the bank watchman, who mistook Service for a burglar. Explanations followed, but instead of retiring for a drink or other repairs to his nerves, Service wrote about a shooting: "A bunch of the boys were whooping it up in the Malamute Saloon." Hours later he finished what was to become the most declaimed of all verses of the North, a lurid, exciting ballad of unrequited love and vengeance entitled "The Shooting of Dan McGrew."

Service's second ballad, "The Cremation of Sam McGee," was inspired by a colorful yarn he heard at a party. It concerned a man who cremated his pal, and it had a surprise climax that occasioned much laughter from the men who listened with Service. The young bank clerk, thunderstruck, did not join in the hilarity: "I had the feeling that here was a decisive moment of destiny," he wrote. "I still remember how a great excitement usurped me. Here was a perfect ballad subject." He hurried away from the party and walked into a nearby woods. Under the brilliant moonlight, a line popped into his head: "There are strange things done in the midnight sun," and this line was followed by verse after verse. "For six hours I tramped those silver glades, and when I rolled happily into bed, my ballad was cinched. Next day, with scarcely any effort of memory I put it on paper. . . . Though I did not know it 'McGee' was to be the keystone of my success."

The poet's next inspiration came as he was looking down at Miles Canyon near Whitehorse. Taken with the grandeur of the scenery a line came to him: "I have gazed on naked grandeur where there's nothing else to gaze on." Before his walk was over he had hammered out a complete poem, "The Call of the Wild." Inspiration followed over the next two months as he wrote "Spell of the Yukon," "The Law of the Yukon," and many other poems. He did not think the world was waiting anxiously for his verse, but he did invest $50 in printing a little book. Soon his printer wrote with startling news. Before the type had been set, 1,700 copies had been ordered after reports spread about his exciting book.

Service's *Songs of the Sourdough* appeared in 1909 and has not been out of print since.

Historic Attractions: Steamboat. The town's history as a river transportation center is well represented by the riverboat SS *Klondike*, which is docked in the center of town near the Robert Campbell Bridge. (The bridge is named for the famed Hudson's Bay Company fur trader. See pages 65–68.)

Mile 866.2: Whitehorse International Airport

The airport, to the east of the highway, was built during World War II.

Historic Attraction: Transportation Museum. The Yukon Transportation Museum has an interesting collection of exhibits, including pioneer aircraft, steamboats, and old vehicles that traveled the Alaska Highway.

Jack Dalton's Country: Whitehorse to Alaska Border

The Alaska Highway is miles and miles
of nothing but miles and miles.
— *U.S. soldier*

Jack Dalton explored the country between the headwaters of the Yukon River and the coast of Lynn Canal for several years to determine the best approaches to the interior. (See Mile 53.5: Champagne for a site associated with Dalton.) In 1890–91 he guided an expedition sponsored by the *Frank Leslie Illustrated Newspaper* along the trail that the Chilkat Indians used for trade with interior tribes. E. J. Glave, the expedition leader, and Dalton explored the Alsek River on their return journey to the coast. In 1891 Glave and Dalton took the first pack-horses from Pyramid Harbor on Lynn Canal to Lake Kluane.

In the following years Dalton, anticipating the eventual discovery of gold in the interior, built trading posts at Pyramid Harbor, Pleasant Camp, and Dalton House (a mile upstream on the Tatshenshine River from Neskataheen). He also improved the old Chilkat route to establish the Dalton Trail as a toll road for prospectors bringing pack animals into the Klondike, charging $2.50 per horse and $2 a head for cattle. It was by way of the Dalton Trail that the first livestock reached Dawson City during the gold rush. In 1898 he established the Dalton Pony Express for freighting into the interior, using 250 horses purchased in Oregon to provide rapid mail and passenger service. This enterprise failed when the White Pass and Yukon Railway put steamboats on the Yukon River.

The Chilkats did not welcome Dalton's intrusions on their trade route. Earlier they had burned the Hudson's Bay Company's Fort Selkirk, to the discomfort of trader Robert Campbell. And they had harassed prospectors who began using the Chilkoot Pass into the interior in the 1880s. The U.S. Navy intervened several times to keep the Chilkoot Pass open. Dalton had to face the Chilkats without such help, although he did have allies in the Stick Indians of the interior, who saw that having a white trader established in their country lessened their dependence on the Chilkats. The Chilkats tried to thwart Dalton by stealing two caches he had left on the trail for his return from the interior in 1895. Dalton barely made it to a third cache. In 1898 he also survived an attack by Chilkats. It was widely reported in Dawson that he had been killed, but it was his assailant who died.

Dalton's feud with the Chilkats had already led to violence and his prosecution for murder. In March 1893 he heard that young Daniel McGinnis, the cannery storekeeper at what later became Haines, had been advising the Chilkats about Dalton's plans to use their trail for trade. Whether McGinnis had been making gratuitous mischief or feared trade rivalry, he acted foolishly in antagonizing Dalton. Dalton burst in on him, demanding: "What do you mean talking to Indians about me, about my going to the interior?"

As the frightened storekeeper professed ignorance of the charge Dalton ordered an Indian interpreter to repeat what other Indians had heard from McGinnis: "Jack Dalton is going in there," said one Indian, "and make a trading post and then we get poor." After a further exchange of words McGinnis tried to get out of his chair, and Dalton smashed him on the head three times with his revolver. The gun fired, and McGinnis fell with a fatal wound.

Dalton had been serving as a deputy U.S. marshal for the region, which made his killing of the storekeeper seem even more offensive to other Alaskans. Feeling in Juneau ran high against him when he went on trial for murder. Folks in Juneau were not sympathetic about Chilkat threats against Dalton, even though he testified that the Indians had threatened to kill the first white man who went into the interior "whether Jack Dalton or not." Dalton, a sturdy, powerful man, also testified that McGinnis, at 120 pounds, had threatened him with an axe. To the outrage of most people in Juneau, the jurors acquitted. The federal prosecutor believed that Dalton's attorney, John Maloney, had bribed some of them, but it was not proven.

By the time of the gold rush this unfortunate affair had been largely forgotten. Dalton's achievements during the gold rush and subsequently in mining, exploration, transportation, and other commercial activities made him something of a legend. In 1915 a Seattle newspaper described him as "easily the first citizen of Alaska," one in whom Alaskans had "absolute faith."

After the first phase of the gold rush, the Dalton Trail was not much used. In 1943 the U.S. Army revitalized much of the old route in constructing the Haines cutoff from the Alaska Highway between Haines and Haines Junction.

The attention of Canadians to places associated with Jack Dalton is notable because his fellow Americans have not honored his memory, despite his outstanding achievements in several regions of Alaska. Indeed, the United States government once withdrew the honor of a placename, renaming Dalton Glacier, one of the ancient, powerful frozen rivers of ice that flow into Disenchantment Bay, northeast of Yakutat.

Israel Russell of the U.S. Geological Survey had recognized the accomplishments of Jack Dalton as a trailblazer and prospector in 1891. He recommended that the glacier be named for him. When the Juneau grand jury later charged Dalton with murder, Russell asked the government to rename the glacier for John Henry Turner of the U.S. Coast & Geodetic Survey. No doubt Turner was a capital fellow, but he was not as significant in northern history as the man whose name was erased in his favor.

If you look at Alaska's most used reference work, Donald Orth's *Dictionary of Alaska Place Names*, you notice that the Dalton Highway from Fairbanks to the Arctic was named for Jack Dalton's son. Nothing is named for the senior Dalton, whose achievements have not been surpassed by any other pioneer.

Mile 887.1: Historic Cairn

On April 1, 1946, the U.S. Army turned over the administration of the Alaska Highway to the Corps of Royal Canadian Engineers. Eighteen years later, in 1964, the federal Department of Public Works took over highway maintenance in Canada from the Canadian army engineers. A cairn in front of the NorthwestTel complex commemorates both of these transfers.

Mile 894.8: Junction with Klondike Highway 2

Highway 2 takes travelers to Takhini Hot Springs while Alaska-bound drivers swing west for Alaska.

Mile 889.1: Loop Drive

A three-mile drive on an old section of the Alaska Highway starts at this point.

Mile 905.4: Old Dawson Trail

A point-of-interest sign indicates the old Dawson City winter stage-coach route. Earlier travelers from Whitehorse to Dawson City took this trail when steamboat transportation was not available, stopping along the way at the numerous roadhouses. Here the route crossed the Takhini River. The route was used until 1950, when the Mayo-Dawson road (Highway 2) was opened to traffic. The old route has not been maintained.

The Excitement of Dawson City. Almost everyone bound for the gold field wanted to get to Dawson City, the boomtown near the initial gold strike of 1896. Named for Canadian geologist George Dawson, the town was the center of excitement and a place where everyone hoped to make a fortune. But living there was expensive. Meals cost $2.50 in 1897–98, a time when a hungry man could fill up for fifty cents in the states. A very hungry man in Dawson might spend up to $10. In restaurants and homes the flapjack was a popular standby. "It is the glory of the Klondike and appears in the most remote and impoverished diggings," noted a visitor. "Always palatable, it is, in the language of the miner, 'tough, but filling.'" Of course, rich men wanting a treat ordered fresh fish in season, savoring the disparity in taste, texture, and novelty between fish and flapjacks and the other stand-bys, beans and salt pork.

By January 1898, there were about 6,000 people in the Canadian Yukon, including 5,000 at Dawson and nearby camps. Of these, 75 percent were Americans. Another 1,000 whites were in the Alaska Yukon, most of them stranded en route to Dawson. Over the 1897–98 winter and early spring, about 28,000 argonauts crossed the Chilkoot and White passes, and 5,000 to 6,000 started upriver from St. Michael. Alfred H. Brooks has estimated that two-thirds of those who started from St. Michael failed to reach their goal for various reasons. Overall, only 34,000 of 60,000 stampeders reached the Klondike. By the close of navigation in 1898, 30,000 people were left in the Yukon, 13,000 of whom were in the Klondike and 4,206 at Dawson. An estimated 35,000 people disembarked at Skagway and Dyea in 1897–98: 5,000 at Wrangell for the Stikine River route, 3,000 at Valdez for the glacier route, 1,000 on Cook Inlet, and 2,000 on all-Canadian overland or river routes. If each of the estimated 60,000 stampeders had only two backers or family members contributing—a conservative estimate— then over 200,000 people "had a more or less direct financial interest in the gold rush."

Over the fall of 1896 miners mushed or walked to the Klondike. Most of them came from the Fortymile region, where the closest community of miners was located. The stampede from Circle, then the largest population center in the interior, did not get under way until January 1897.

Fortymiler Joe Ladue is generally considered Dawson's founder because he shipped in his sawmill and laid out the town site. William Ogilvie, the Canadian boundary surveyor, arrived soon to make an official survey of Ladue's site and of the rich creeks, Bonanza and Eldorado, where gold discoveries had been made. With these preliminaries accomplished, the place boomed as wild-eyed arrivals kept coming.

Men kept busy over 1896–97. The town lacked amenities, but all the stampeders brought in their own provisions, so there was food enough. Nonetheless, the arrival of the first steamboat from downriver in July was a great event. Food had been getting scarce, and the liquor had long since run out.

As the summer advanced more stampeders came in from various Yukon camps, and, increasingly, argonauts from the outside hit town. By the close of navigation, Dawson held 5,000 souls and was well provided with saloons, dance halls, and gambling places.

A year later the town had 30,000 people and was one of the most celebrated places in the world. And, thanks to the Mounties, who had been on duty early after moving in from their base at Fortymile, Dawson was a secure, orderly community. A man could drink and gamble all he wanted and hire a prostitute, but he could not display a weapon or indulge in rowdiness without police interference. In early camps on the American side of the boundary, such as Fortymile and Circle, miners' meetings kept order reasonably well, but that system would never have worked in a camp of Dawson's size.

Dawson was a town full of Americans forced to observe the laws of Canada. Miners complained about Canada's laws and government officials. They hated the tax of 10 percent on their gross gold production (the first $5,000 was excluded), but they paid it.

Dawson boomed from 1897 to 1899. Its prosperity ensured that the Yukon Territory would no longer be the scarcely populated realm of a few scattered fur traders and Native Americans. Because many of the placers in the Klondike region were quickly worked out, however, Dawson City could not sustain its prosperity. The Nome rush in 1899 came when Klondike opportunities were declining. Much of Dawson's population rushed to Nome, but Dawson still remained the important mining, supply, and cultural center of the upper Yukon.

The stampede to Nome continued in 1900, and then, within three years, excitement shifted to Fairbanks. Production fell sharply in Dawson and the Klondike as drift mining methods became less productive. But there was plenty of gold left for the investors who brought in advanced technology. With the advent of hydraulic and dredge mining on properties consolidated by Arthur Treadgold, the industry revived and prospered until 1914. In fact, of the $250 million in gold produced in the Klondike, 75 percent was mined after 1900.

Characters of Dawson City. Among the best-known Klondike characters of Dawson's heyday were a handful of show business promoters who entertained at the Opera House, Monte Carlo, Palace Grand, and other houses. Dawson's first theater, the Opera House, was built of logs, with a bar and gambling room in the front and the theater at the rear. Benches accommodated those who bought tickets at fifty cents; more expensive boxes ringed the area. Drinks cost double the bar price in the boxes, but these murky places assured some privacy. Tallow lights served for box lights in the first theater. The splurge of building by the summer of 1898 brought new, more fitting structures, featuring gaslights, chair seats, nice dressing rooms, and other furnishings appropriate to the boomtown's status.

Swiftwater Bill Gates's entry into the theater world owed something to his friendship with Jack Smith. Both men had made big money on claims, and Smith persuaded Gates to back his Monte Carlo theater. Gates went down to San Francisco to hire dance hall girls, summoned reporters to his Palace Hotel suite, and told them colorful stories.

Becoming a character in Dawson was not all that easy. Among the rivals were skilled showmen and such vastly experienced self-promoters as Captain Jack Crawford, a veteran frontiersman and so-called poet-scout who sold goods and told lively stories from his store, the Wigwam. Crawford offered fine prospects to men foolish enough to invest in the Captain Jack Crawford Alaska Prospect and Mining Corporation. Another frontiersman-showman was Arizona Charlie Meadows, a legitimate theater man who built the Palace Grand.

The dance hall women, particularly those who managed to marry or otherwise attach themselves to newly rich men, competed with theater owners to create their own legends. Performers' salaries were as much as $150 weekly, and women could earn nugget tips and other remunerations. Because salaries and other costs were far above those faced by managers outside, there were no profits unless oceans of booze were dispensed and gamblers flocked to the gaming tables.

In 1899 Arizona Charlie Meadows opened the Palace Grand, a magnificent house by any standard, seating 2,200. Folks were impressed and showed their approval by howling like dogs at the July opening. One feature of the opening season was a play based on Meadows's own adventures as a scout with Al Sieber in the Geronimo campaign. On stage he rescued a fair damsel tied to a stake by Apaches and escaped in a theatrical tour de force, plunging with his horse from a fourteen-foot elevation into eight feet of water. Before going north, Meadows had been associated with Soapy Smith of Skagway fame in Cripple Creek, Colorado. Meadows promoted a bullfight while Smith, then known as the Denver Bronco Kid, ran a gambling concession stand.

One of the most interesting aspects of Dawson's theaters was their dramatic treatment of local characters and events. Swiftwater Bill Gates's edge in the race to legend was fostered by lively skits highlighting his adventures. *Still Water Willie's Wedding*, produced at the Palace Grand, was one of several dramatic efforts to make fun of Gates by playwright-actor John Mulligan. *Still Water* later had a revival at the Tivoli Theatre, where it was greeted with "yells of delight and amusement."

Kate Rockwell, later "Klondike Kate," was a latecomer (1900) to the Dawson stage, and her paramour, Alexander Pantages, was a poor waiter at Dawson until he borrowed money to establish the Orpheum Theatre. Later, Pantages left to foster a grand scheme for a circuit of vaudeville houses and made millions with the Orpheum network. Kate made her modest theater reputation as Klondike Kate after leaving Dawson with Pantages and got big headlines when she sued Pantages for breach of promise in 1905.

Mile 914.7: Takhini River Bridge

The Takhini River's name is derived from the Tagish Indian word *takh*, meaning river. Many northern placenames show the same redundancy in repeating the Native American and English words.

Mile 926: Fire Site

A point-of-interest sign describes the great forest fire of 1958, when 1.5 million acres were ravaged after campfires started the blaze.

Mile 927.3: Kusawa Lake

Kusawa Lake, formerly Arkell Lake, is reached by a turnoff here. This large lake, forty-five miles long and two miles wide, in the coastal mountains was initially reached by an access road put through by Alaska Highway builders so they could harvest timber for bridge construction in 1942.

Mile 936.8: Mendenhall River Bridge

The Mendenhall River was named for Thomas C. Mendenhall (1841–1924), superintendent of the U.S. Coast & Geodetic Survey.

Mile 939: Mountain Views

From this point travelers can see three prominent mountains to the north, including Mount Bratnobor, named for an English mining prospector and promoter who was involved in Alaska's Wrangell–St. Elias region. Alaskans would not have named a mountain for him because he derided mining prospects and thwarted a boom. Mount Kevin and an unnamed peak are the other two peaks in sight.

Mile 953.5: Champagne

Champagne is the pleasant name once given to a camp on the Dalton Trail leading to Dawson City (see introductory essay to this chapter). According to legend, Jack Dalton's employees celebrated their successful cattle drive to Dawson at this point with a carefully preserved bottle of French champagne. Whatever the truth, the name stuck; even local Indians are known as the Champagne Indian Band. Their cemetery is located here.

Because it was on the Dalton Trail, the camp gained more substance after a gold rush to Bullion Creek in 1902 and a boom at Burwash Creek in 1904. Harlow "Shorty" Chambers built a roadhouse and trading post to serve the region in 1902.

Mile 965.6: Aishihik River Bridge

The Aishihik River Bridge and a turnoff to the Canyon Creek Bridge are at this point. The Canyon River Bridge was a pioneer structure built by the Jacquot brothers in 1920 to move freight and passengers across the Aishihik to Silver City on Kluane Lake. From Silver City boats conveyed freight and passengers to Burwash Landing. The army rebuilt the bridge in 1942. Its most recent rebuilding was in 1987.

Geological Features. The Ruby Range bordering the north side of the highway from Aishihik River to the Kluane River is underlain by Triassic granodiorite and Jurassic-Cretaceous biotite schist, gneiss, and amphibolite. Prospectors have searched the streams of the Ruby Range for gold but with only limited success.

Mile 977.1: Kluane National Park Ice Field

A turnout with information plaques describes the Kluane National Park Ice Field, which is visible from here. Canada's highest ice field, said to be also the world's largest alpine ice field, occupies the center of the park. Mount Kennedy, named for President John Kennedy, and Mount Hubbard, named for Gardiner Hubbard, the first president of the National Geographic Society, are visible behind the front range. The peaks tower almost 15,000 feet and form part of the Wrangell mountain border between Canada and Alaska.

The ice fields visible from this point are outstanding examples of the many glaciers that can be observed in the Rocky Mountains, the St. Elias Mountains, the Wrangell Mountains, and the Alaska Range along the route of the highway. Glaciers form in areas of heavy snowfall as permanent ice fields, which move like rivers over varying distances. Glaciers have periods of surge and of retreat. Retreating or melting glaciers dump the sediment they have been carrying, including sand, gravel, and rocks of all sizes and types. The resulting moraine becomes a conspicuous feature of the area.

Mile 986: Haines Junction

This is the junction of the Alaska Highway and the Haines Highway (Yukon Highway 3). The port of Haines, 150 miles to the south, is an important feeder line to the highway and a terminal of the Alaska Marine Highway. Haines Junction was established by army engineers in 1942 to support construction of a branch highway to Haines for the transport of construction and military materials from Lynn Canal. This access to Haines gave the military a backup port to Skagway for defense needs.

Kluane National Park. The headquarters of the Kluane (kloo-WA-nee) National Park is located at Haines Junction. The park is virtually a wilderness, and the history of its creation is closely related to the history of the highway. Robert G. McCandless, author of *Yukon Wildlife*, tells of the conservation efforts of U.S. Secretary of Interior Harold Ickes during the road construction period. In July 1942 Ickes had just given federal government protection to eight million acres of the Wrangell–St. Elias region by withdrawing it from public entry. The vast tract would not finally be designated a park for many years and would precipitate strenuous battles between conservationists and developers, but Ickes took advantage of highway construction to prevent private appropriation of the land for mining or any other purpose "pending definite location and construction of the Canadian-Alaskan Military Highway."

Ickes then wrote T. A. Crerer, his Canadian counterpart, "I am informed that the Canadian-Alaskan Highway will touch or make fairly accessible, several fine areas within British Columbia–Yukon wilderness. You of course are familiar with them. The Tuchodi Lakes–Toad River region is highly scenic and has exceptional game resources, including grizzlies, Osborne caribou, Stone sheep and the most northerly herd of elk. In the same general area is the Liard canyon. West of Whitehorse, from Kluane Lake to the Alaska boundary are the highest mountains in Canada and some of its most famous wildlife."

Ickes went on to explain that trumpeter swans in the United States were devastated by development and that the highway threatened them and other wildlife in Canada. Ickes understood that the war emergency might be followed by an ecological one unless both governments seized the moment. He called for "a uniform policy of conservation along the Highway now and for the future."

Canadian officials shared Ickes's view. James Smart, comptroller of parks, initiated the long process that would result in the creation of the park thirty-five years later. Protecting the land in the interim by withdrawing it from public entry took only four months. The government dispatched Charles LeCapelain to Whitehorse to help safeguard all of the land and wildlife affected by highway construction.

Today Canada and the United States still cooperate in preserving this great wilderness region. Kluane and Wrangell–St. Elias rangers meet often to formulate common policies, a sensible proceeding, since wildlife does not observe borders.

Along the highway you may hear disparaging comments on either side of the border about restrictions within the parks and the "interference" of government with the "old ways." Some of the complainers are not very old, yet they have a bitter tone. To most of us in Canada and the United States it seems reasonable that their so-called right to exploit public land must be balanced with the rights of others and their children. A region without parks can be very depressing. Anyone who has ever driven through Texas, where public lands passed from federal to state domain at statehood and then swiftly into private hands, will understand what I mean. It is said that Texans brag a lot, but despite the state's huge expanse, I have never heard them boast about their extensive parks.

Kluane was first set aside as a game sanctuary and was established as a park in 1972. Its official boundaries were set in 1976.

Mile 991.4: Lookout Place

Up the hill just off the highway is an information sign concerning the area's geological features. (See pages 51–55 for a general description of geological features of this region.)

On the south side of the highway, west off the bridge over Bear Creek, a fifteen-mile trail to Sugden Creek commences. Rock hounds will find much of interest along this way. At mile eight of the trail, outcrops of peridotite lie in an intrusion along the mountain slope on the west side of the Dezadeash River. Crystals of green olivine measuring three to four inches in length may be discovered. Placer deposits in the area have been worked for gold.

Mile 1,000.1: Bear Creek Summit

Bear Creek Summit, at 3,294 feet, is the highest point on the highway between Whitehorse and Fairbanks.

Mile 1,013.6: Kluane Range

To the west the Kluane Range is in view; the highway parallels it to the north from Haines Junction to Koidern. Between the impressive chain of eight thousand-foot peaks are glacier-cut valleys and numerous rivers. West of the Kluane Range is the Duke Depression, a narrow, deep trough that divides the Kluane Range from the St. Elias Mountains.

Mile 1,019.8: Boutillier Summit

Travelers get their first glimpse of Kluane Lake from this point. Fossil plant pollen indicates that Kluane Lake dates from 30,000 to 65,000 years back. Such pollen is evidence of plants and the feeding habits of Ice Age mammals, including the woolly mammoth. Plants like those growing here now once grew near the lake. Although the climate of the Shakwak Valley was colder 30,000 to 65,000 years ago, the area was ice free.

Mile 1,020.3: Ruins of Silver City

A road to the east takes travelers 3.1 miles to the mouth of Silver Creek and the ruins of Silver City, a trading post and police barracks that was located on a wagon road from Whitehorse to the Kluane mining district. Gold was originally discovered in 1903. For a time placers were worked south of the highway at Sheep, Bullion, Burwash, and Arch creeks and the Koidern River. By 1905 the shallow placers were largely worked out, although some mining continued for several years.

Mile 1,027.8: Slim's River Bridge

The highway begins its winding, thirty-nine-mile passage along the west shore of Kluane Lake. Slim's River, which empties into the lake here, shows the movement of glacial silts that were driven by strong mountain winds off the glacier, then carried downstream by the river and dumped in the flats near its mouth as the current slowed its pace. The silts extend the river delta into Kluane Lake, creating dry mud flats that fill in this end of the lake.

Along the shores of the lake, rock hounds can find pebbles of red chert or jasper, which originate in the Permian Skolai terrane rocks of the Wrangell Mountains.

Mile 1,029: Sheep Mountain

In 1989 the government opened a new visitor information center that provides information and displays on the flora and fauna of Kluane National Park. Sometimes mountain sheep can be spotted on the slope from this point.

Mile 1,029.1: Soldier's Summit

This was the site of the official opening of the highway on November 20, 1942. The band played "God Save the King" and "The Star-Spangled Banner." Speeches were made. It was a great occasion but rather cold for outdoor ceremonies.

Dignitaries represented the Territory of Alaska and the Dominion of Canada, the United States, and the U.S. Army. Among the speakers was Col. K. B. Bush of the U.S. Army Corps of Engineers, who insisted that "this road will rank for all time among the greatest engineering feats the world has ever seen."

Gen. James A. O'Connor of the U.S. Army spoke of Canadian trappers, gold seekers, and farmers of the region, and of the forests, rivers, and mountains through which the highway passed. The highway, he said, "was the end of pioneering," signaling the close of a long chapter of history. "For those of us who have had a share in its construction, the Alcan Highway will be an indelible memory."

The most interesting speech was that written by Interior Secretary Harold Ickes and read by another Interior Department official. Ickes, a liberal statesman of daring and purpose, expressed a beautiful vision for the highway in the speech. To him it seemed that the road could be a realization of democratic ideals. "I see it as the Little Man's Road," he said, "the road where Mr. Jones and Mr. Ivanovich and Mr. Chang will help each other fix a flat. I see it leading from the factories and gleaming white houses of America across to Siberia, Asia and Europe into the houses of all those native and minority races, those men and women who must be granted the same rights and privileges we ask, if ours is to be a free world."

Fifty years have passed since Ickes emphasized the potential influence of the highway on geographic barriers. At about the time the road opened to civilian traffic, a frigid political breeze—the Cold War—froze the Bering Sea and Bering Strait tighter than any winter ice. Now a great thawing is under way. Alaska and Siberia are being linked by the narrow Bering Strait. People are going back and forth as never before in history. Scheduled airline flights are also available for the first time. It seems that we have the chance to allow people, trade, and ideas to flow easily and naturally between northwestern North America and northeastern Asia without undue political interference: a realization of Ickes's dream.

Twenty-five years after the highway's opening, the event was commemorated with another ceremony here. Notice was taken of the speed of the 11,150 troops and 7,500 civilian workers; the 233 bridges (many already replaced by large culverts by 1967); the first year's construction costs of almost $20 million; and the $20 million or so that was being spent annually in the 1960s for maintenance of the highway.

An old prospector's cabin, built in 1905 by Alexander Fischer, is across the highway from the highway-dedication monument.

Mile 1,040.4: Congdon Creek

Congdon Creek was named for a miner, Frederick T. Congdon, a stampeder from Nova Scotia in 1898.

Mile 1,051.5: Destruction Bay

Destruction Bay was a highway construction camp of tents erected in 1942. After the commanding officer had all the trees cut down, a savage storm ripped through the camp, causing general havoc, hence the place's name. Some people have argued that the name refers to a storm that upset boats full of Klondike stampeders as they rounded the point on the lake.

After highway construction the place became a maintenance facility, around which a small settlement developed. Tourist facilities also developed because of the lake and local recreational opportunities.

Burwash Landing (Mile 1,061.5)

Burwash Landing, reached by a short turnoff, is a resort and outfitting place for Kluane National Park. It was named for Lachlin Taylor Burwash, the recorder at Silver City in 1903.

The original trading post was established by Eugene and Louis Jack-quot, two brothers who prospected in the region and, seeing the potential of Kluane Lake for sportsmen, became hunting guides. They married local Indian women and were among the best-known residents of the region for decades.

Kluane Lake, forty miles long and two to six miles wide, is the largest lake in the Yukon Territory. Major rivers that drain through the lake en route to the Bering Sea are the Donjik, White, and Yukon.

The Kluane Museum of Natural History is on the east side of the highway.

Murder! Iris Woolcock, who wrote an account of the trip she made to Alaska and back to the states in 1948, was driving south when she heard about a local incident of violence. As an independent, single woman, Iris was drawn to other women who broke away from conventional marital arrangements. She called at the home of Annie Haydon, an Indian woman who had just come back from Whitehorse, where she had been prosecuted for murdering her husband.

"There was a nice spot to park my trailer in front of Annie's house," Iris noted in her account. "I pulled in just as she was arriving from the bus. Thinking she might not have much food in the house, I stepped across a lot of blood and brains on the threshold to offer her some cans of veal stew."

The women hit it off immediately. Annie invited Iris for supper and conversation, which turned on grisly recent events thrilling to the visitor. "I had to look at that threshold once in a while," Iris wrote, "to make myself believe I was enjoying the hospitality of an honest-to-goodness murderess." Annie's son came to report having seen a big brown bear in the area. Annie was annoyed because the Mounties had not given her back her rifle, the trusty 30.06 that kept the family supplied with their meat, furs, and hides. Annie admitted that she was a sure shot "and it was a quick shot from the 30.06 that dropped her husband on the threshold as he re-entered the house after one of their quarrels when he had cuffed her around and given her a couple of bad scratches on the wrist. She had enough of such treatment."

Iris sympathized: "I suppose you'll be much happier now without him."

"Oh yes," Annie replied, "I don't know why I ever put up with him for thirty years."

"He must have been pretty mean to you," Iris said.

"He was mean," said Annie. "He knock me around and he all the time talk mean. He think I know nothing. He never have no love, no kindness. He didn't know what happy family could be. He just drug himself up. I like to go see my relatives. He never let me. He drag me off up here and marry me when I thirteen years old."

After leaving Annie, Iris visited with Rube Chambers, the local game warden. Rube said that everyone loved Annie, but he wondered at the court's wisdom in finding justifiable homicide and letting her go free. "It might have been well," he reflected, "to give her a couple of years just to keep too many women from thinking they might so readily bump off their husbands." Rube may have been strict about husband shootings because he was a married man himself. Iris did not comment on his attitude except to note that the "men are a dime a dozen in this country."

Folks told Iris about another murder in the area. A woman killed a man with an axe. When the judge asked her why she did it, she said he backed his truck into her clothesline and ran her nice white sheets into the mud after a hard day's wash. The woman was angry, and she picked up the nearest thing handy, which happened to be an axe, and let fly with it.

"Dismissed," said the judge, who must have been a clean-sheets man.

But Iris did not want to leave the impression that all Yukon women were a threat to human life. She praised Mrs. MacIntosh, a Mountie widow, who ran a little trading post at Bear Creek and was gentle and kind to everyone. In her seventies, she still did all her own work.

Mile 1,066: Williscroft Creek

Williscroft Creek is named for Walter Williscroft, a Canadian highway engineer, who started work on the highway in 1943 and was in charge of maintenance from Whitehorse to the Alaska border from 1945–50. Sometimes, when washouts were extensive, Williscroft was kept on the run day and night. He recalled one occasion when "I never had my boots off for a week." In a Kluane Lake slide of July 1945 a Cat was buried by mud and the driver thrown into the lake, but Williscroft was able to save him.

Mile 1,067: Duke River Bridge

The Duke River was named for George Duke, an early miner. The Duke River Valley, a wide gap in the Kluane Range, is visible from the south side of the highway. Of geologic interest is the Amphitheater Mountain, on the other side of the gap, which is in the foreground of the Donjek Range. Its flat cap of Tertiary Wrangell basalt overlies sedimentary strata. Below the lava cap are coal seams and fossil leaves, evidence that helps date the rise of the St. Elias Mountains.

Mile 1,078.5: Wellgreen Nickel Mines

To the west you can see buildings of the Wellgreen Nickel Mines, owned by Hudson Bay Mining and Smelting Company. The nickel deposit was discovered in 1952 by Wellington Green. After considerable investment operators produced ore in 1972–73, some forty tons of which was shipped by truck to Haines for shipment outside for smelting. As the costs were high and the deposit proved none too rich, the mine was closed in 1973.

Mile 1,083.5: Monument

A monument to an American soldier who died in 1942 while working on the highway.

Mile 1,084.6: Kluane Village

Here one can view the distant peaks of the St. Elias Mountains, including Mount Kennedy, Mount Logan, and Mount Luciana. Mount Logan, at 19,520 feet, is the highest peak in Canada.

Mile 1,100: Donjek River Bridge

When the U.S. Army engineers reached the Donjek River in 1942, they had to span an impassable mud flat stretching over three miles and cut by seven wide river channels. They built seven separate wooden bridges for the channels, which served their purpose for several years. In 1952 Canadian army engineers built a permanent steel bridge that crossed eight channels over its length of 1,600 feet. The eight spans were constructed outside, then shipped by sea to Skagway and by rail to Whitehorse, then carried on sixty-ton trucks from Whitehorse to the river.

From Burwash the highway follows the Kluane River. To the north can be seen morainal ridges of sand and gravel, which lie between the Kluane and Donjek rivers. The Donjek River originates in the Donjek and Steele glaciers. The Steele Glacier surged 1,600 feet in one month in 1966.

Mile 1,135.6: White River Bridge

Robert Campbell, the Hudson's Bay Company trader and explorer, named this river for its color, which is produced by the heavy sediments of white volcanic ash in the water.

Geology of the Region. On the east side of the White River a mining road leads to the Canalask Mine, where copper, lead, zinc, and nickel were produced. The Canyon City copper deposit is accessible from this road; you can also see where the huge copper nugget, 2,590 pounds, now at the McBride Museum in Whitehorse, was located. The copper slabs weathered out of fractions in the Triassic Nicolai basalt. Indians made utensils and weapons from the local copper, and these items became important for trade with Tlingits, who lived on the coast.

A layer of white volcanic ash, a pumice that looks like white sand, is widespread in the southern Yukon, forming a layer of several inches to two feet beneath the topsoil. It usually mantles lower mountain slopes and can be seen as a thin layer beneath topsoil on lower ground and in road cuts and cutbanks of streams and rivers. Sometimes the ash is found in fragments as long as four inches.

The ash resulted from a volcanic explosion near the Natazhat Glacier, thirty miles southwest of the White River Bridge, 2,000 years ago. Near the glacier are dunes of ash several hundred feet high. With the eruption winds carried the ash to the Yukon, spreading it north along the Yukon-Alaska border into the Ogilvie Mountains and east into the Mackenzie Mountains.

Mile 1,143.3: Sanpete Creek Bridge

Sanpete Creek was named by an early prospector from Sanpete County in Utah. From the bridge the highway leaves the Shakwak Valley for the Yukon Plateau, which extends all the way to Dawson City. The Shakwak Valley continues northwesterly into the Nutzotin Mountains and Alaska.

Mile 1,150.3: Chisana Gold Rush Marker

The historical marker describes the Chisana gold rush of 1913, one of the last northern gold stampedes. The Chisana is a tributary of the White River; the town, founded during the stampede, is now within the boundaries of Alaska's Wrangell–St. Elias National Park. The rush was singular in drawing miners from Whitehorse and Dawson City via the White River as well as from Fairbanks and Cordova. After two seasons most of the 2,000 miners left, and the town declined.

Mile 1,168.5: Beaver Creek

Beaver Creek was one of two connection points for highway construction crews working from the south and north in 1942. The connection in October 1942 allowed vehicles to travel the entire route because the other connection, at Contact Creek, had been made in September.

Festivities celebrated the opening of the highway in late 1942, but the ninety-mile section from the Donjek River to the Alaska border did not remain open. The troubles builders had had in the summer of 1942 with permafrost, the White and Donjek rivers, muskeg, and swamps had not been resolved. With the 1943 spring thaw trucks were mired in the mud all along the highway. By summer the road was in such terrible shape that it was nearly impassable by men on horseback, and no vehicles moved on it.

The Utah Construction Company established some temporary camps in the area but could not set up a permanent camp or move in heavy equipment during the summer. Float planes brought in men and light equipment, and heavier equipment came in gradually as workers restored sections in sequence.

By this time the builders knew how to protect the permafrost. Instead of removing ground cover insulation, they left it intact and dumped rock and gravel over it. The pace quickened with the cool fall weather and the opportunity to use heavy equipment. The crews working from the north met those working from the south at Beaver Creek on October 13, 1943. Workers conducted a modest opening ceremony, celebrating the first time since winter of 1942 that the highway was open all the way.

The Canada Customs Station was located at Beaver Creek until 1983, when it was moved several miles north of town.

Mile 1,170.5: Canada Customs Station

The new Customs Station here was built in 1983.

Governing Alaska:
The Alaska-Yukon Border to Tok

"And how do you like Alaska, Sarge?"
"You mean goin' to or comin' from?"
"I mean standing still."
"No opinion."

—*The Big Road*

Contrary to what is commonly said about the purchase of Alaska by the United States in 1867, Americans were generally pleased with Secretary of State William Seward's initiative. Territorial expansion to the north was favored, and the price was low. It seemed strange that Russia would give up a huge territory when Europeans customarily fought bloody wars over portions of land that could be tucked unnoticed in any corner of Alaska. And Alaska, according to the proponents of its acquisition, was a veritable treasure box of wealth in furs, fisheries, timber, and minerals. Senator Charles Sumner of Massachusetts enthused in Congress over "forests of pine and fir waiting for the axe; then the mineral products, among which are coal and copper, if not iron, silver, lead, and gold." To William Seward, Alaska seemed certain to be "the great fishery, forest, and mineral storehouse of the world."

Neither Sumner nor Seward really knew the extent of Alaska's mineral and other resources at the time of the acquisition. Much of the territory had not yet been explored. Speculation about great wealth was not unreasonable, but constraints of climate and distance delayed development until actual mineral discoveries caused widespread excitement. Only gradually did the emphasis shift from furs to gold, but the traders did open the interior and support the early prospectors, who patiently probed streambeds for signs of gold.

Early Trade

Russian efforts to develop trade in the interior began with the establishment of posts at St. Michael in 1833 and Nulato in 1839. The Nulato post remained the farthest inland and farthest north throughout the Russian period, but other posts were founded at the mouth of the Unalakleet River and at Andreesvsk, Alexkseevsk, and Komarovsk within a few years. Russian Mission (Kvikhpak) on the lower Yukon was established in 1845.

Alaska's fur possibilities also stimulated the Hudson's Bay Company to establish Fort Yukon in 1847 at the mouth of the Porcupine River, a poaching on Alaskan territory that lasted until Capt. Charles P. Raymond of the U.S. Army protested the boundary matter to the great British company in 1869. Raymond had been dispatched because of complaints from American traders and had voyaged to Fort Yukon from St. Michael on a small trading steamer. After his survey confirmed Fort Yukon's American location, Raymond notified the HBC men and raised the stars and stripes over their post. Raymond reported cautiously on the economic potential of the Yukon: "Profitable management requires fixed posts. . . . There is no place for small enterprise." Whether the length of travel justified large investments "remains to be seen." As for gold, "no valuable mineral deposits in workable quantities have been found in the vicinity of the Yukon River up to the present time." This report was not quite accurate, as Frederick Whymper of the Western Union Telegraph Expedition had reported on signs of gold near Fort Yukon a few years earlier.

Raymond's flag raising was a necessary gesture, but his assertion of American authority was not fortified by other government action. Many years would pass before the United States presence in the interior was firmly established. The government's indifference to the Yukon through the 1870s can hardly be wondered at, since it was impotent even in parts of the West, where serious Indian-white conflicts brewed.

With the acquisition of Alaska in 1867 the potential of the fur trade attracted several American companies, including the Pioneer Company, Parrott and Company, Taylor and Bendel, Faulkner and Bell, the

Jansen Company, and the Hutchinson, Kohl Company. The latter became the Alaska Commercial Company (ACC) and dominated the Alaskan trade for decades. A lease arrangement secured the ACC a monopoly over the lucrative Pribilof Island fur seal harvest, but elsewhere in Alaska other traders were free to compete.

The role of the federal governments of both the United States and Canada has been of paramount importance in this region's history. Executive and legislative actions taken thousands of miles away affected matters of law and order, economic development, and the pace of self-government.

Law and Order

The U.S. federal court system was in place when the Klondike gold rush started, but only in southeastern Alaska. The first court in the interior was not established until 1900. During the 1897–98 turmoil the only U.S. marshal was based at Juneau, and the corruption of his deputy at Skagway and of a U.S. commissioner at Dyea allowed Soapy Smith to continue his lawless ways at Skagway.

From 1886 the influx of miners into the interior created an urgent need for law enforcement. By 1895, Circle's population was 500, yet the residents had to depend upon the capricious justice administered by miners' meetings to settle civil disputes and sanction criminals. Though the "pure democracy" of the miners' meeting came to be praised by pioneers in later years, the system was imperfect and sometimes intolerable.

A deputy marshal was sent to Circle in 1897, but he stopped at Dawson to mine gold and did not even reach his duty station. It was not until spring of 1899 that a regularly appointed deputy settled in Circle. During the turbulence of the gold rush, officers of the U.S. Army were forced to keep order on the Yukon, and the task was beyond their capacity. The lawlessness at Skagway and tardiness in establishing law and order in the interior constituted an unpleasant blot on the government's record. It should be said, however, that the judicial system operated with reasonable fairness and efficiency except in the short-lived instances cited here.

The Mounties

The North-West Mounted Police, or Mounties, were established in 1873. In that year the Canadian force was organized to drive American whiskey traders out of Alberta and police the huge western provinces Canada had recently acquired from the Hudson's Bay Company.

During the gold rush, the Mounties exerted iron control over the teeming town of Dawson City and the Klondike region. Interestingly, this effectiveness came partly because of Johnny Healy, the same American whose whiskey trading had induced the government to form the North-West Mounted Police in 1873. Healy had been one of the first to alert Ottawa to the need to police the new gold fields in the early 1890s. Ottawa responded to Healy's call for police, and the force was on hand when the Klondike was struck; it was able to control the rapid boom of Dawson City and keep order on the trails.

Despite the general acclaim for the Mounties' performance in the Klondike, there were some critics. The American missionary Hall Young reported that Mounties handling the mail conducted a brisk market for those wishing special treatment in the mail line. For an ounce of gold or a $5 bill a police mail clerk would quickly get letters to impatient customers. Young considered the reverence for the police misplaced. "I am not wanting in respect for that heroic body of men," Young wrote, "but after a full experience on the frontiers of Canada and Alaska, I have not witnessed in the United States and Alaska anything in the way of graft that compared with the insolence, rank dishonesty and disrespect for the rights of men which I observed among the officials of the Yukon Province of Canada, and even in the mounted police."

More serious graft charges were brought against leading officials, including Thomas Fawcett, the gold commissioner, and James Walsh, commissioner of the Yukon. Walsh, a former Mountie, had an inflated reputation in Canada for alleged bravery in handling Sitting Bull when the Sioux fled across the American border to escape U.S. Army troops. Since Sitting Bull was anxious to convince Canadians that he was a peaceful fellow, Walsh's courage was never tested. At Dawson Walsh's reputation suffered from allegations that Walsh's cook got his job only after agreeing to give three-quarters interest in any mining claims he located to Walsh or his brother. Since Walsh was in a position to gain inside information on Dominion Creek claims, this revelation was damning.

After two months in office Walsh was removed. So was Fawcett, whose grafting was evident. The government did not bring Walsh to trial, either to avoid embarrassment or because sufficient evidence of corruption was lacking. William Ogilvie, the honest Canadian government surveyor who replaced Walsh, believed that the Walsh brothers were crooks. Nonetheless, the government later named one of the lofty peaks of the St. Elias Mountains after Walsh.

Ogilvie and his successors restored public confidence in the government, and the Mounties have continued to keep order in the Canadian portions of Alaska Highway country into the present time.

Aiding Development

The U.S. government did aid northern development, but not enough to satisfy Alaskans. Pioneers wanted heavy investments in transportation, services, and other areas and complained that government assistance efforts were tardy, ill defined, parsimonious, grudging, inefficient, and indifferent to Alaskans' needs.

Historian Clarence L. Andrews observed that the national wave of conservation in the first decade of this century included a laudable effort to protect Alaska's resources from wasteful exploitation. Coal and oil lands were withdrawn, and forests and wildlife habitat preserves were created. Unfortunately, these protective measures halted development. The private builders of the Alaska Central Railroad from Seward to the interior and the Copper River Railroad from Cordova to Kennecott stopped construction of lines to the Matanuska coal mines and Bering River coal deposits, respectively. Depression gripped the land. The Alaska Central Railroad faltered after laying seventy-nine miles of track, and the Alaska Syndicate did not consider carrying the Copper River and Northwestern Railroad beyond Kennecott. In response to the clamor from Alaskans, the government authorized a public railroad in 1914, taking over the Alaska Central's track and the thirty-nine-mile short line of the Tanana Valley Railroad near Fairbanks.

Once the railroad builders started work, Alaskans were certain that their mining future would be prosperous. They liked to quote the character in Rex Beach's novel, *The Iron Trail*, who wailed that without transportation "the riches of Alaska are as useless today as if hidden away in the chasms of the moon." What Alaskans still had to learn was that transportation, for all its importance, was only one factor in the development equation.

Construction of the Alaska Railroad did not provide the economic stimulation that backers had yearned for. Progress was slowed by

World War I; completion was deferred until 1923. Even then the government did not go after traffic with the aggression that James Hill showed in developing his Great Northern Railroad. Hill subsidized colonization, aided farmers, and laid tracks to mines, whereas the government did little to promote the Alaska Railroad and mining. Alaskans believed that government delays in opening the coal lands prevented their development, although in truth it was determined that better coal could be mined at lower cost elsewhere in the nation.

Similarly, when Alaska's population fell sharply between 1910 and 1920, from 64,356 to 55,036, Alaskans blamed the government. The decline continued into the 1920s, and Alaskans echoed the pleas made by Governor Thomas Riggs in 1919: "Unless the government pursues a more liberal policy . . . the territory can never reach that stage of productiveness for which there is every possibility."

Miners did get help during the dark days of the Great Depression. In 1933, the price of gold, long fixed at $20.67 per ounce, was increased to $35. Gold production leaped immediately from $9,701,000 in 1933 to $16,007,000 in 1934, rising to $26,178,000 by 1940. Actual output over the 1933–40 period rose from 469,286 ounces in 1933 to 749,943 ounces in 1940. But the recovery proved to be short-lived because World War II forced the closure of most mines in Alaska. Mining did not revive much after the war. Some Alaskans continued to blame the government, but after statehood those old cries had a hollow sound.

The government was slow in providing civil governance, adequate land legislation, and effective services before 1899. The government was also slow in exploring, surveying, and providing for the needs of Native Americans. In the gold era, however, the response to Alaska's needs came swiftly. Exploration, the enactment of civil and criminal codes, postal services, military protection for and assistance to destitute prospectors, and telegraph and trail building were among the achievements of the period.

Local government was not established for some years, and Alaskans complained about the quality of services, but most of their requirements were attended to.

Alaskans found the tie-up of coal land from 1906–12 inexcusable, and many accused the government of favoring the exploitations of the Alaska Syndicate. And Alaskans were unanimous and vociferous in their insistence that the government do more to aid economic development.

The government's responsibility to provide law and order, civil government, and essential services is clearer than its obligation to encourage development with specific projects. While the government had always fostered road and railroad construction, it did not respond generously or quickly enough to the demands of Alaskans. Even if it had, however, it could not have provided the kind of progressive development Alaskans yearned for. Government help alone would not create viable mining and other industries.

Alaska's growth following the doldrums of the mining industry came because of defense spending during World War II and in the years following. Federal expenditures were huge for the Alaska Highway and other roads, airfields, and military bases. Government and government-sponsored payrolls filled the economic vacuum in the economy left by the decline of mining. With these benefits and population increases, Alaska was deemed to be ready for statehood, which was achieved in 1959.

Unlike Alaska, the northern Canadian territories did not come by purchase, although much of the Northwest had been the charge of the Hudson's Bay Company until the mid-nineteenth century. Northern Canadians were as vociferous as Alaskans in demanding federal assistance in services and development. The sparse population of the Yukon Territory after the decline of mining made it easier for the Canadian government to justify its stinginess toward public works projects.

Mile 1,189.5: The Alaska-Yukon Border

The highway crosses the 141st meridian at this point. Canadians have no trouble with the 141st meridian as a boundary but are still mad that fixing the border along the coast in 1904 excluded the possibility of a Canadian port of entry to the interior. Controversy raged among diplomats for years as earlier Russian and British agreements were debated; the decision favored American occupancy of the Panhandle. Canadians think that British diplomats, who then conducted their international affairs, sold them out, and that President Teddy Roosevelt was far too aggressive in pushing American claims.

Whatever the merits of the old argument, the boundary surveys of the 141st meridian, which began in 1907, were conducted amicably by parties of Canadian and American surveyors, initially led by Clyde Baldwin for the United States and A. J. Brabazon for Canada. Thomas Riggs, later a governor of Alaska and still later a critic of Gen. William

Hoge's work on the Alaska Highway, was an original member of the American team, and eventually its leader.

Surveying was not easy because much of the area was mountainous, and there were only two places on the meridian—crossings of the Yukon and Porcupine rivers—where water transport was possible. Everywhere else parties depended upon packhorses, which never moved faster than two miles an hour and could not be worked more than six hours daily. With mosquitoes and gnats, travel was tough in high summer, but working into the autumn was harder yet. As Riggs noted, it was a season "when ice is thick enough to just break through with the weight of man, when the wolves howl around the camp, when in the morning huge fires must be built to thaw out tents and pack-rigging, while packers freeze their fingers tying packs on the dejected and shivering ponies."

Summer seasons lasted 100 days, and the men worked every day from 6 A.M. to 6 P.M. Riggs stayed on the job for five years and boasted of making "the straightest of the world's surveyed lines." The parties cut twenty-foot-wide strips along the route—even including dense forests—mapped the region, and placed border monuments at intervals. The route stretched 600 miles from Mount St. Elias to the Arctic Ocean.

Riggs and the others finished the survey in 1912. In writing about the venture, Riggs described what the men had gained beyond the work itself while traveling in the North. "There is an unexplainable fascination about the North," he wrote. "The very hardships lend a paradoxical charm. The vast solitudes, uninhabited and lonely, have an irresistible call."

Climbing the high regions of the St. Elias Mountains, where the boundary line runs between the great Kluane and Wrangell–St. Elias national parks, were the most rigorous excursions, but the men enjoyed the beauty of the country. Other northern scenes impressed Riggs, such as a splendid display of the aurora. "I will never forget my last night out from Lake Kluane," he wrote in 1909. "It was clear, cold, and still. The Northern Lights started as a low white arch across the horizon. They grew brighter and brighter, turned to color. Soon the entire heavens were carved with the most grotesque whirls and eddies of all the colors of the spectrum, suddenly appearing and disappearing. I have never seen anything like this."

The surveyors were in the field when the Chisana gold rush of 1913 brought stampeders from Dawson City, Whitehorse, Cordova, Valdez, and Fairbanks. Had the Chisana gold field been wealthier, the history of the White River country near the highway would have been different. As it turned out, the Chisana field was virtually worked out after a couple of seasons, and the brisk traffic into the White River country slowed.

Mile 1,189.5, Historical Mile 1,221.4: The International Boundary

From this point on to Fairbanks *The Milepost* log switches from driving distance to existing roadside mileposts for northbound travelers. The two standards of measurement reflect the highway straightening that has been going on since its construction. The driving distance between Dawson Creek and the Alaska border is thirty-two miles less than it was originally. Thus the mileage listed here would be 1,189.5 (the actual driving distance) if we had not switched to the original distance signposts when we crossed the border.

The International Boundary Commission, composed of officials from Canada and the United States, oversees the maintenance of the border strip, which includes periodic clearing of the six-foot-wide swath. The boundary runs from the Arctic Ocean to the North Pacific along the 141st parallel except for the Pacific coastal section.

Mile 1,221.8: Port Alcan

Northbound travelers must pass through the U.S. Customs Station here.

Paving Controversy. On this part of the highway drivers used to ponder the obstinacy of the Canadian government over the matter of paving. From 1954 some Canadians urged the Department of Public Works to take over the Canadian portion of the highway from the Department of National Defense. Defense did not give highway improvement and paving a high priority. Alaskans wanted another joint Canadian–U.S. effort on paving and commissioned a project study in 1961. The study estimated paving costs at $103 million and indicated that tourism gains and economic developments would recover the expenditure. Canada was not ready to move but did make the administrative transfer to the Department of Public Works in 1964.

British Columbia maintained the first 84 miles of the highway even before this transfer. From 1972 the Yukon Department of Highways maintained the Yukon section. British Columbia argued that it was not responsible for the northern B.C. section but contracted maintenance out to private contractors. Squabbling went on about paving and who would pay. A study commissioned by the Canadian government in 1966 found that paving would not be economically feasible but recommended bridge and road improvements.

Dust-ridden travelers complained about Canada's shortsightedness, and in 1973 the United States offered to pay for paving the Haines Road and the highway northwest of Haines Junction. Canada did not refuse this generous offer. The paving and improvement was done over an extended period.

By the mid-1980s Canada had contributed to the paving of one-third of the highway in Canada and a treatment of the rest to reduce the dust. In the years since more paving has been done, particularly when the governments began preparation for the fiftieth anniversary of the highway. It is likely that travelers in 1992 will cover virtually the entire highway on paved surfaces.

Mile 1,240.3: Dealing with Permafrost

The permafrost that caused highway builders such exasperation in 1942 is still a factor in road maintenance. Experiments are made regularly on devices that may reduce the effects on the highway of permafrost thaws. Here highway engineers have made vertical culverts on both sides of the road in the hope that they will prevent frost heaves.

Mile 1,243.6: Geology of the Region

A sign provides some natural history information. Among the prominent sights are dunes of sandy loess, a fine deposit of glacial silt found in much of the interior, including the Tanana Valley.

The highway follows the flank of the Nutzotin Mountains, which are to the southwest. The Alaska Range, extending into central Alaska, is the dominant mountain range along the highway. Its eastern end forms two masses, the Mentasta and the Nutzotin mountains. Both are composed of Jurassic and Lower Cretaceous marine sedimentary and volcanic rocks of the Nutzotin belt that extend from the eastern Alaska Range to an eastern boundary against the Denali Fault in the Yukon. Scattered outcrops of Nutzotin belt rocks known as the Dezadeash group are found between Dezadeash Lake and the Yukon-Alaska border.

Fossils are rare in the Nutzotin belt. In the section between Chisana and the boundary rocks are gray mudstone, siltstone, and muddy sandstone. In the upper part of the section is the Chisana formation, consisting of andesitic rocks that erupted both beneath the sea and on land and are exposed near Nabesna and elsewhere.

Evidence indicates that in the late Jurassic period, 175 million years ago, a sinking basic occurred in the Nutzotin belt. At some time between 150 and 100 million years ago rocks of the Wrangell Mountains were folded, uplifted, and deeply eroded. Volcanic eruptions produced the andesite of the Chisana formation.

The highway follows the Denali Fault from the border to Northway Junction, where it can be traced to the south. Basically, the fault is a discontinuous north-facing bluff of sedimentary deposits, displacing glacial moraines from the last Ice Age. The fault sweeps in an arc from the Queen Charlotte fault system in southeastern Alaska across the Canadian border, back into Alaska through the Alaska Range, and westward to the Bering Sea coast.

Mile 1,256.7: Yarger Lake

The magnificence of Alaska's mountain ranges are well viewed from here. To the south, the St. Elias Mountains; to the southwest, the Wrangell Mountains; to the west, the Mentasta Mountains of the Alaska Range.

Mile 1,263.5: Chisana River

The highway follows the Chisana River and passes by numerous ponds, suggestive of the many beavers that first brought white men into the country.

Mile 1,264: Northway Junction

Northway is an Indian Village with a population of 364 located seven miles south of the highway. It was named for village chief Walter Northway, who adopted the name of a trader and riverboat skipper early in this century. In the summer of 1991, Chief Northway was recovering from hip surgery. On Easter Sunday he had slipped and fallen on the ice in the village.

Chief Northway may be the world's oldest living man at 114 years of age. He was born in 1876 at Moose Creek and maintains an active interest in his village.

Northwest Staging Route. Northway was one of the sites on the Northwest staging route for which an airport was built during World War II. Ferrying aircraft over the Northwest staging route to the Soviet

Union during the war was a huge contribution to the struggle against the Germans. The Americans first suggested that lend-lease aircraft be sent to Russia in September 1941. Joseph Stalin believed that the route would be too dangerous and favored the shipping route by sea to Murmansk.

After Pearl Harbor the American military was in a desperate hurry to send military equipment to Alaska and requested permission of Canada to use the bases along the Northwest staging route. With Canada's approval the Americans decided to use the route for ferrying planes to Siberia as well and contracted with Northwest Airlines for support services. Northwest sent personnel to Edmonton, Fort St. John, Fort Nelson, Watson Lake, and Whitehorse, where they performed station maintenance, using Canadian facilities.

Crashes were common along the route in the early months of its use. In one 1942 operation, thirteen expensive B-26 bombers started for Alaska from the states. Before reaching Fairbanks, four crashed in what became known as the Million Dollar Valley in the Yukon.

For ferrying aircraft Fairbanks was selected as the turnover point. Russian crews gathered there to take over from the American fliers and transport their planes northwest to Nome and across the Bering Strait to Siberian bases. Over the following three years 8,000 combat and transport planes were delivered to Fairbanks and turned over to the Russians. Before flying the planes the Russian pilots were instructed at bases at Big Delta and Fairbanks.

Mile 1,284.2: Tetlin National Wildlife Refuge

The village of Northway is within the Tetlin National Wildlife Refuge, consisting of 950,000 acres. The refuge was established in 1980 along with new parks created in the same legislation. Extending west from the Canadian border and south from the Alaska Highway, it is a region of rolling hills, the Nabesna and Chisana rivers, and hundreds of ponds providing nesting places for waterfowl. The huge population of nesting waterfowl each season was a deciding factor in the preservation of the area. Officials estimate that 90,000 ducks are hatched each year. Larger nesting birds include sandhill cranes, arctic and common loons, ospreys, bald eagles, and ptarmigans.

The refuge is also the home of wolves, foxes, moose, bears, coyotes, and beavers. The Visitors Center at Mile 1,229 provides information on the refuge and its uses.

Mile 1,301.7: Tetlin Junction

The highway is within the Tetlin Indian Reserve in this region. One in southeastern Alaska and the Tetlin Indian Reserve are the only two Indian reservations in Alaska. The reserve was created through the efforts of John Hajdukovich, a trader who had posts among the Upper Tanana Indians at Carcross and other locations. Hajdukovich showed a concern for Native Americans and was anxious to protect them from whiskey traders. The creation of the reserve gave the people the power to expel any such traders. (See Mile 1,431 for more biographical information on Hajdukovich.)

Taylor Highway and Eagle. The Taylor Highway (Alaska Route 5) heads northeast to Eagle from this junction. Eagle was once an important center: the seat of the first court in the interior, established by Judge James Wickersham in 1900, and the site of the U.S. Army post of Fort Gibbon. It was also the U.S. Customs Station for all steamboat traffic on the Yukon passing from or to the Yukon Territory, just a short distance upriver. Eagle can be reached by fast riverboats from Dawson City during the summer tourist season.

The Taylor is a summer dirt road to Eagle on the Yukon River. Travelers can take the Taylor to Jack Wade Junction and turn east onto the Top of the World (Yukon) Highway for Dawson, 78.8 miles distant. The 161-mile highway was named for Ike Taylor, chief engineer of the Fairbanks District for the Alaska Road Commission (the Highway Department is now a division of the state's Department of Transportation). At Taylor's urging construction on the highway started in 1946 and was completed in 1954. The highway opened a passage into a region of great historic significance for mining.

Ernie Pyle's Story from Eagle. Ernie Pyle traveled to the Yukon and Alaska in the summer of 1937 and brought his talent to bear on that already colorful region. He was one of the nation's most popular newspaper reporters in the 1930s and 1940s, with a keen eye for good stories and a way of telling them that attracted a diverse body of readers. It was at Eagle that Pyle wrote the famous story about Nimrod's teeth. He claimed that he had heard it as he traveled north from Seattle as well as in Whitehorse and Dawson and that all Alaskans talked about Nimrod. Perhaps the story did have wide local standing, but Ernie Pyle conveyed it to the larger world.

According to the standard story, Nimrod was a tough but toothless Alaskan woodsman. To remedy his handicap he killed a bear, installed the bear's teeth in his own mouth, then ate the bear. Pyle refuted some aspects of the episode. He discovered that Nimrod was not a primitive Alaskan but "a cultured gentleman from Maine," a miner who had suffered from scurvy in 1905 and lost his teeth. Nimrod gathered replacements from mountain sheep, caribou and, for the molars, a bear. An experienced artisan, "he made a plate of aluminum, drilled holes for the teeth, set them in, and then worked the warm aluminum back over to hold them tight. It took him a month. He made two sets, uppers and lowers. And he wore them for nearly twenty-five years."

A Seattle dentist exchanged standard dentures for the interesting ones Nimrod wore and displayed them in his office. Nimrod assured Pyle that "he ate a lot of bear meat with them, but not the bear the teeth came from."

Pyle's style is well expressed in his conclusion to the Nimrod story: "Nimrod has been outside Alaska only once in forty years. He probably will never go again. But forty years of isolation have not corroded him. He is still just as polite, just as gay, just as neat, just as gentle, as he was the day he arrived hoping to make a thousand dollars.

"And so he sits in his little shop—the man with the dreams to do fine things, but who achieved fame by putting the bear's teeth in his mouth—he sits, still telling you of what he is going to do someday."

Mile 1,303.4: Tanana River Bridge

The Tanana River has its origins in the Wrangell–St. Elias National Park glaciers that create the Chisana and Nabesna rivers. The two rivers form the Tanana near Tetlin Junction. The Tanana is now a tributary of the Yukon River, but there is evidence that before the Pliocene era the valley was drained by a stream flowing northwest into the Copper River, thence to the Pacific Ocean.

The highway follows the Tanana River all the way to Fairbanks via Tok and other places described in the following chapter.

On to Siberia:
Tok to Fort Wainwright

Glory road moving
How far do you go
Finish your miles
More miles to go.
 — *The Big Road*

Among the many railroad schemes involving the Northwest, the one concerning the great road to Siberia is especially interesting in the history of the highway.

When you drive the Alaska Highway, you are on the road to Siberia and beyond to Moscow, Paris, and the other great cities of Europe. For some years early in this century promoters had a vision of linking the continental United States and Europe with a railroad that would cross the Bering Strait by bridge or tunnel. When I see the end of the rail tracks leading north at Fort Nelson, I listen hard for the faint whistle of the grandest ghost railroad of them all — the Trans-Alaska-Siberian Railway, a project envisioned by William Gilpin, Johnny Healy, and others.

Don't be surprised if the Alaska Highway is extended to Siberia in the future or a railroad is built along a parallel route. You could push on from Fairbanks to the Seward Peninsula and cross over the Bering Strait. Nothing to it with a bridge or tunnel, and now the political climate is favorable. It is only 44 miles, about the same as the Panama Canal's length, between Cape Prince of Wales, Alaska, to Cape Dezh-

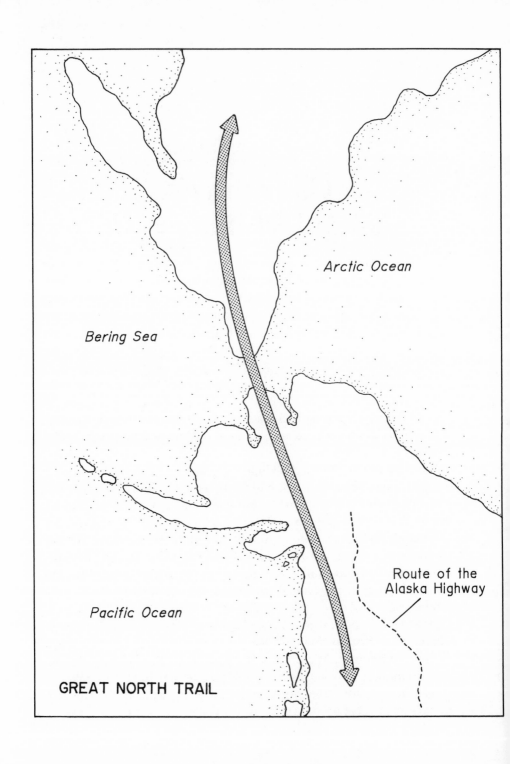

Arctic Ocean

Bering Sea

Pacific Ocean

Route of the
Alaska Highway

GREAT NORTH TRAIL

neva, Siberia, and this short stretch is broken by the American island of Little Diomede and the Soviet island of Big Diomede.

In 1849 William Gilpin started publicizing the need for a North American–Siberian railroad. In 1861, when he was governor of Colorado, he amplified his ideas in a book entitled *The Cosmopolitan Railway: Compacting and Fusing Together All the World's Continents*. None of the American transcontinental railroads had been completed, but the Russians were building their trans-Siberian railroad, so the plan seemed practical to Gilpin. He argued that progress demanded a railroad "that would help unite all the world's people in peace and prosperity."

Gilpin's plan seemed more feasible in 1865, when the Western Union Telegraph Company tried to link the continents by telegraph across the Bering Strait. This major survey and construction project occupied crews dispatched to northern British Columbia, the Yukon River valley of Alaska, and northeastern Siberia. The Alaskan party included William Healy Dall and other scientists recommended by the Smithsonian Institution who did valuable scientific work while the project lasted. In 1867, around the time of the purchase of Alaska from Russia, the telegraph project was abandoned. Western Union had succeeded, after several failures, to lay a telegraph cable across the Atlantic. With the Atlantic cable in operation, there was no need to continue the expensive job of bringing a wire across the North to the Bering Strait and to Siberia.

Gilpin was not the only railroad enthusiast. Congress asked J. W. Powell of the U.S. Geological Survey to investigate a route. Powell recommended an extension north from the Northern Pacific railroad route in Montana, through Alberta to the headwaters of the Peace River, thence to the headwaters of the Yukon River—a route that approximates that of the Alaska Highway. From the Yukon Powell's route would have run over to Grantley Harbor on Seward Peninsula and across the Bering Strait.

Interest in the railroad was stimulated by the northern gold rushes, especially as American prospectors started finding good prospects in Siberia. But it was all talk until John J. Healy got involved. Healy, one of the North's great entrepreneurs, had been a modest trader at Dyea on Lynn Canal when he planned and obtained backing for his North American Transportation and Trading Company in 1892. He put a fleet of steamboats on the Yukon River and built a number of trading posts several years before the Klondike gold discovery. He would have made a fortune during the stampede except for the fierce competition offered by the pioneer Alaska Commercial Company and other traders who jumped into the Yukon trade. Disappointed with their profits, other stockholders forced Healy out in 1900. Johnny got busy on other schemes, including the Trans-Alaska-Siberian Railway.

Healy tried to get investment money for the railroad in New York and other financial centers. Backers were reluctant to come forward unless the czar approved and agreed to lucrative concessions for the builders. Healy's partner spent months negotiating with the czar's ministers. At one point the ruler approved of the project, and Healy, despite poor health, led a survey party from Dawson City to the White River country in 1906. But then the czar changed his mind, fearing the intrusions of foreigners. The rail scheme collapsed.

Mile 1,314.2: Tok

Tok, a construction camp in 1942, has become one of the more important places on the highway as a service center for Alaskan state and federal agencies. Population is 1,200, with 3,600 in the greater area. It was named after a local Indian village, Tok Hakate—a name recorded by Russian traders on mid-nineteenth-century maps.

Blackened areas along both sides of the highway approaching Tok from the south are evidence of how close the town came to destruction by the huge forest fires of 1990. Residents were forced to evacuate for a time, and highway drivers were not permitted to stop. In the summer of 1991, residents earned money picking morells for outside suppliers. A profusion of these gourmet mushrooms sprang up following the fire.

Travelers can benefit from a visit to the Alaska Public Land Information Center, where there are natural history and history exhibits as well as brochures.

Tok in 1946. George Hayden of Anchorage kept a highway log for a trip in 1946 that provides a good contrast with modern travel conditions. Among the places he was grateful to reach was the bustling service center of Tok. Hayden, his wife, two sons, and a male friend piled into a 1941 Ford station wagon for their November trip. They had taken the rear seat out of the wagon and replaced it with a double mattress that rested on top of their luggage. Also packed were a complete camping outfit—including tent and gas stove—skis, rifles, a pistol, fishing poles, tools, extra gas and oil, and three spare tires. Gear was also packed in a rack on top of the wagon, which loaded weighed about four tons gross.

It was not an easy trip. They started from Anchorage, where the temperature was twenty degrees above zero and the ground was free of snow, and headed for Palmer. Just out of Palmer Hayden broke a drive shaft and had to be towed back for repairs, which took several days and required sending back to Anchorage for parts.

With repairs done, the Haydens drove to Gulkana through blowing snow, staying at the Santa Claus Lodge. Departing at noon, the party soon had more adventures: "We slid off the road on a sharp curve and made the brush at 1:30 P.M. No damage. Tom and I walked five miles back at the Gakona roadhouse to get a truck." Returning, the men found that a wrecker had already come along and pulled the Ford back on the road, charging only two dollars. "The kids were pretty cold after sitting in the car for a couple of hours, so we decided to go back and spend the night at Gakona instead of going on to Tok." The group reached Tok at 4 P.M. on November 6. Gas at the Northern Commercial Company store cost 55 cents a gallon. Tok appeared to Hayden to have a bright commercial future. "This looks like a good spot for a roadhouse," he noted. "I look for quite a land rush around this junction next summer."

Moving on, Hayden's party reached the Alaska Highway at 6 P.M. Alaskans were not spoiled in the matter of highways, and Hayden was impressed by the new road. "It sure looks wide. The best road I have seen in over five years. In most places it would make a three-lane highway and any place two large trucks can pass."

Mile 1,317: Mukluk Land

Though the recreation park is not of historic significance, its gateway originally held a huge sculptured image of a mosquito. This seems an appropriate place to consider the mosquito in northern literature.

Alaskans like to commiserate with one another about the winter's numbing cold. But at heart they know that winter is a pleasant season. After all, there are no mosquitoes in winter.

If you ponder this trade-off during a period when your blood is being consumed drop by drop while a buzzing cloud of mosquitoes swarms all over you, you get the point. Winter is blessed with comparative peace and quiet and may be the healthier season.

Among the wildlife in the North no creature has been the subject of more literature than the mosquito. Comparatively, lynx, beavers, moose, caribou, wolves, rabbits, and even fearsome bears have been neglected. Books may try to frighten you by relating encounters with bears, but every true northerner knows that the really scary stories involve mosquitoes.

It is proper to begin with the first census of Alaska, made by Ivan Petroff in 1880, which could be considered official notice of the problem. Ivan did not try to count the mosquitoes, but something about the heartfelt tone of his comments conveys his sense of the hopelessness of the odds: "There is a feature of this country which, though insignificant on paper, is to the traveler the most terrible and poignant affliction he can be called upon to bear in the new land. . . . Language is simply unable to portray the misery and annoyance accompanying [the mosquitoes'] presence."

The census taker in 1890 also took official notice of the pest, arguing that mosquitoes dimmed the joys of the prospectors' experiences: A region "might contain the most beautiful scenery in the world or the richest mine, but the clouds of mosquitoes obscured their vision and occupied their attention to the exclusion of everything else."

Jack London tried to be lighthearted in some of his journal entries: "Badly bitten under netting—couldn't vouch for it but John watched them and said they rushed the netting in a body, one gang holding the edge while a second gang crawled under. Charlie swore that he has seen several of the larger ones pull the mesh apart and let a small one squeeze through. I have seen them with their probosces bent and twisted after an assault on a sheet iron stove."

Another keen-eyed pioneer reported seeing two mosquitoes fold down the wings of a third and push him through the fine mesh of a head net.

Miner Bob Medill studied mosquito tactics to find the best defense. The insects, he believed, always circled about one's head from left to right. "The circle is about two to three feet in diameter, and a foot thick. The center six to eight inches is so dense one can not see through it. Desiring to see each other, two persons must lower or raise their heads suddenly and peer below or above the circle."

How could anyone be certain that a traveler on the Alaska Highway near Watson Lake in 1946 was exaggerating when he described giant mosquitoes "as big as hummingbirds, thick as fog, and forever hungry"?

We understand the helplessness expressed by Johan Jacobsen, an early scientist voyaging on the Yukon River, in describing "the plague" attacking him. "One can overcome dangers, and against ambushes one can protect oneself with vigilance; accidents can often be prevented or lessened by energy and quick action; one can overcome all kinds of situations, but against the relentless pursuit during waking and sleeping carried on by mosquitoes, which are constantly replaced by millions of new ones, there is no defense."

Taking some joy in the battle—however futile—is perhaps the best tonic against despair. Prospector I. Banta reported with spirit on his campaign: "Fought mosquitoes to the finish, grand retreat, am returning in disgrace, killed about forty million but they still come on not daunted."

Early on all northern travelers realize that swearing may provide psychic relief for a moment but that the most eloquent, vehement words have no real effect. Nor does violent action. Stampeder Ed Morgan watched as his partner swung his knife at surrounding clouds of mosquitoes, "thrusting, jabbing, and crosscutting through the swarm like a cavalryman." After the man tired, he inspected his knife, rejoicing at the bloodstains and body fragments. The body count ran into the hundreds but—alas—the mosquitoes still came on.

History has recorded many examples of breakdowns among afflicted men. One veteran was amused when a tenderfoot he traveled with ceased to scoff at the bug menace and collapsed in a heap, uttering "a bitter wail." Other reporters have observed that "strong men have been known to give way and cry like babies as a result of bites."

One of the familiar stories of early gold camps related the use of mosquitoes as police. Miscreants were stripped naked and placed unguarded in a mosquito-proof tent. The prisoners did not have to be watched further.

Geology Along the Highway. From Tok to Fairbanks the highway follows the Tanana River, passing hills of Precambrian schist intruded by Cretaceous granite. To the south of the road from about fifty miles south of Delta Junction, sand and gravel predominate and extend from the south bank of the Tanana River all the way to Fairbanks. This outwash plain reaches to the Alaska Range. Along the highway the sand and gravel are especially noticeable on the first few miles west of Delta Junction. Large, rounded cobbles form part of the heavy load of sediment carried by the Tanana and its tributaries.

When driving from Tok to Delta Junction, the rock you see is late Precambrian to early Paleozoic, with some intrusive younger (Mesozoic) granite. The rocks near Delta Junction are overlain by Pleistocene sediment deposited by the Tanana River. Prominent granite bluffs include Cathedral Bluffs, twenty-five miles west of Tok and across the river from the highway, and Tower Bluffs, further west on the north side of the river. Fifty miles north of Delta Junction there is the Shaw Creek Fault. The rest of the way to Fairbanks rocks are late Precambrian to early Paleozoic metamorphic types of the Yukon-Tanana terrane.

The Yukon-Tanana terrane contains the oldest rocks in Alaska, recrystallized sedimentary rocks that were deposited 2.2 billion years ago, when the region was at the edge of the continent, hundreds of miles to the south and east. They were faulted to their present location.

Mile 1,325.8: Tanacross Junction

Tanacross, a village of the Tinneh Indians, is reached by a short loop road from the highway. The Tinneh, like all the other Indians of the highway region, belong to the Athabaskan language group.

Earlier Tanacross was known as Tanana Crossing. In 1901–02 trader and railroad promoter Johnny Healy proposed a railroad from the coast at Valdez to Tanacross. He was so confident of success that he encouraged trader E. T. Barnette to establish a trading post there. Barnette, however, could not get his little river steamboat high enough on the Tanana River to reach Tanacross. Instead, he stopped on the Chena River, which became a lively place when Felix Pedro discovered gold in the area. Soon Fairbanks became the leading boomtown of the region.

Mile 1,361.3: Dot Lake

Dot Lake is a small Indian village and headquarters for the Dot Lake Indian Corporation. Settlement began in the 1940s, after highway construction; a school was established in 1952. The Dot Lake Chapel was built in 1949.

The missionary church at Dot Lake is one of many in Alaska serving Native Americans. Historically, the missionaries have been critical of the whites' treatment of Native Americans, whereas many whites have condemned clergymen for their interference.

Hudson Stuck, the far-ranging Episcopal missionary, was a close observer of the natives through the latter part of the stampede era, including the first two decades of this century. His conclusion about the effect of the white miners on the aborigines was unequivocal: They "brought nothing but harm to the native people of Alaska." As one instance, Stuck cited the situation at Fort Yukon during the 1897–98 winter, when 350 Klondike-bound miners were stranded by the freeze-up. The miners spent their time amusing themselves with the natives and their own large stores of whiskey: "There was gross debauchery and general demoralization. It took Fort Yukon a long time to recover from the evil living of those winters and the evil name that followed."

Missionaries were not popular with whites who corrupted natives. They were quick to report violations of the liquor law. At Fort Yukon an indignant steamboat hand remonstrated with Stuck: "Why it's got so . . . that a man can't give a squaw a drink of whiskey and take her out in the brush without getting into trouble!"

Missionaries were generally popular with respectable miners, the lowlife's opinion notwithstanding. Most miners believed in spreading Christianity and the whites' ways among the native people and had no reason to be in conflict with the clergy. There were men, however, who argued that the natives should be free from the influences of missionaries and all the whites. Hudson Stuck addressed this issue on several occasions. He argued vigorously that the Native Americans desperately needed the protection missionaries could give against the depredations of the white riffraff who followed explorers, traders, and prospectors into the country.

The Native Americans most seriously affected by the influx of whites were those who abandoned their traditional pattern of life to live in mining towns. Some were women married to whites, whose children became an integral part of the white community, were educated in the local schools, and found employment within the mining economy. These town natives did not necessarily have a hard lot in making the transition to a new world. Even if the mixed-blood children were denied entry to the upper regions of society, they were, for the most part, treated decently by the white settlers. Other natives dwelled on the fringe of the community, sharing only marginally in its life, living between two worlds and fitting into neither. Their ghetto existence was unsanitary; they were ill housed, likely to suffer from diseases, and often ravaged by alcoholism. Their fate was a visible reminder that the white intrusion had brought disaster as well as prosperity.

But there were only a few scattered mining communities to attract natives, and their number diminished as the gold placers were worked out. The great majority of Native Americans maintained their village existence and avoided close, frequent encounters with whites. For thousands, the handful of missionaries and teachers provided the only contact with the white culture—not that their isolation assured them of a better fortune than town natives. Life for many was a hard struggle for sustenance, as it had always been. Famine and disease were very real threats.

Those who complained of the government's policies toward Native Americans in the North centered their grievances on neglect rather than aggression. But government failures or successes in education, welfare, and medical treatment were generated in Washington, D.C., not Alaska.

Despite newspaper editorials calling for a sound welfare policy, some whites understood that the civilization of the natives, previous to contact with whites, had enabled the aborigines to survive in a harsh land. Sourdough Lynn Smith expressed this consciousness: "When one realizes that four hundred years ago, there were more natives living in Alaska than now [1931]; that they were living off the country without any doctor except their own medicine men and women; and that they had to work out their own salvation—we can take off our hats to them—for their way of life worked." Smith's sentiments were shared generally by whites and were the foundation for their basic respect for the Native Americans, a respect that seems to have been greater than that extended by whites to aboriginal peoples on other frontiers. Such respect of northern people for other northern people derived from a shared experience that took the edge off racial antipathies and blurred the numerous distinctions in customs and manners.

Mile 1,374.4: Robertson River Bridge

U.S. Army explorer Lt. Henry Allen named the river in 1885 in honor of Sgt. Cady Robertson, a member of his party. Allen was the first explorer of the Tanana River. He reached it in 1885 after traveling up the Copper River from the coast.

Mile 1,392.7: Gerstle River Bridge

The river was named by Lt. Henry Allen for Lewis Gerstle, president of the San Francisco–based Alaska Commercial Company, which was the most important commercial establishment in interior Alaska from the 1880s. The ACC had steamboats on the Yukon for summer freight and passenger service and stores at convenient locations. The company got its start soon after the purchase of Alaska, when it gained a lease from the government for the harvest of fur seal hides from the Pribilof Islands. The business was lucrative, but eventually the ACC expanded into the interior, concentrating on the fur trade with Native Americans.

The company was not interested in mineral prospects, fearing that mining would hurt the fur trade, but pioneer store managers helped prospectors with grubstakes, thereby encouraging mineral development. The ACC's commercial dominance on the Yukon received its first major challenge in 1892 when Johnny Healy founded the North American Transportation and Trading Company and established posts and steamboat service. Thus by the time of the 1897 Klondike stampede two experienced commercial entities were on hand to serve the gold rushers, and other trade and transport competitors entered the field in 1898–1900.

Mile 1,396.9: Bison Range

This is the area of the Delta burn, a big fire in 1979, of which signs are visible from the highway. Fires are common in the interior because for all the region's appearance as a green forested land, its sparse rainfall classifies it as semi-arid.

A herd of buffalo imported from the states and established in the area in the 1920s has thrived, but its presence causes pain to local barley farmers. Buffalo like grazing on barley, and keeping them out of the fields is difficult. The battle between farmers and buffalo has been going on for some time. Local efforts to appease the buffalos' appetites with other grain can be seen here in the strips of grain growing near the highway.

Mile 1,403.6: Barley Farms

Since 1978 the state government has fostered barley raising in this region. Alaska made 60,000 acres, divided into 22 farms averaging

2,700 acres each, available to farmers that year. In 1982 another subsidized project provided 25,000 acres, creating 15 farms of 1,600 acres each. Today there are 12,000 acres under cultivation.

The perennial economic problem of Alaska has been the dependence on outside sources for virtually all foods; the barley projects and other agricultural subsidy programs sponsored by the state have been efforts to remedy that problem. If barley could be produced economically, it would stimulate the cattle-raising industry and make meat processing in Alaska a viable endeavor. Unfortunately, the results have not equaled the expectations of planners. Delta farmers have been hurt by bad weather, buffalo grazing, high transportation costs, and a weak local market. Alaska farmers have been unable to raise beef because of high costs and the scarcity of local meat-processing plants.

The current economic distress is not a novelty in Alaska's history. Despite periodic efforts by the government over the last hundred years, few successes in agriculture have been achieved. The tyrannies of climate and distance and the lack of market opportunities (despite recent population growth) keep most farming efforts in perpetual danger of failure.

Mile 1,422 (Mile 266 from Valdez): Delta Junction

Delta Junction was a construction camp on the Richardson Highway in 1919. A small community developed that engaged in highway service and some agriculture. Population today is 1,228, with 4,292 in the greater area.

Delta Junction is the official end of the Alaska Highway, the point where it joins the Richardson Highway. But travelers who reach Delta Junction on the Alaska Highway are generally moving on to Fairbanks, and this guide will also carry on to Fairbanks. Mile post designations here will indicate the distances from Valdez on the Richardson as well as the distances from Dawson Creek, just as the highway signs do.

As the Richardson Highway follows the route of the Valdez Trail built by the U.S. Army early in this century, this is a good place to consider the overall role of the army in Alaska. From 1867 to 1877 the U.S. Army governed Alaska from its headquarters at Sitka; it also had several posts along the southern coast. Aside from one reconnaissance of the Yukon River in 1869, the army did no exploration during this period. After the army administration of the territory gave way to the U.S. Navy, the army's role was limited. The Army Signal Corps was active in making meteorological observations in the Aleutians and in the Yukon-Kuskokwim Delta.

In 1885, Lt. Henry Allen of the U.S. Army undertook a major exploration of the Copper, Tanana, and Koyukuk rivers. But other armed services also contributed to exploration and scientific research before the gold rush. Between 1886 and 1898 the navy and the Revenue Marine Service explored the Selawik and Kobuk river valleys. The Coast and Geodetic Survey made astronomical observations, triangulation, and topographical surveys on the 141st meridian in 1889–90. Another scientist, Frederick Funston, voyaged on the Yukon to make a survey for the Department of Agriculture in 1893.

With the gold rush in 1897 the army sent Capt. Patrick Henry Ray and Lt. Wilds P. Richardson to the Yukon. The officers did what they could to keep order; made recommendations on sites for army bases, which were established within a few years; and proposed a series of exploration ventures. The expeditions were made in 1898 under Capt. William R. Abercrombie on the Copper River and Lt. Edwin F. Glenn on the Copper and Susitna rivers and to Cook Inlet and the Tanana River. Geologists of the U.S. Geological Survey accompanied these expeditions.

In 1899 the army sent Abercrombie to Valdez again to survey a military road to Eagle in the interior. A start was made on a trail through Keystone Canyon and Thompson Pass to the Tonsina Valley that year. Soldiers, limited to hand tools, carved out a ninety-three-mile trail adequate for packhorse travel before the season closed in October 1899.

The government trail from Valdez to Eagle was surveyed in 1899–1900 and built by the army over the next several years. During the construction period, the development of Fairbanks caused a redirection of the line from Eagle to Fairbanks. Building the trail over its 376-mile-course was an expensive and difficult process because of the short construction seasons, the mountainous terrain near the coast, and the Alaska Range. By 1906, the route was good enough to attract a commercial carrier: The Ed S. Orr Stage offered passenger and freight service over the full length of the trail. Improvements continued over the years until by 1920 it could be called a highway and was named for Wilds Richardson, the army officer who directed highway construction and maintenance for many years.

Early in the century, it became obvious that a permanent agency was needed for Alaska's roadwork. For this purpose the government established the Alaska Road Commission to undertake trail and road construction and repair. The Alaska Road Commission's modest budget did not permit construction at a pace speedy enough to please miners, but the agency performed with reasonable efficiency for many years.

Another army explorer of the gold rush era besides Abercrombie was Lt. Edwin Glenn, who explored from Cook Inlet. He traveled northward from the Matanuska, Susitna, Yentna, and Kuskokwim rivers to locate the best route from tidewater to crossings of the Tanana River. His mission was to find a route that would enable the army to service its Yukon River posts from Cook Inlet. Joseph Herron made the first exploration of the upper Kuskokwim River under Glenn's command.

The War Department reorganized its territorial governance in 1900. It created the Department of Alaska with posts at Fort Davis near Nome, Fort Liscum near Valdez, and Fort William H. Seward at Haines. It also established four posts on the Yukon: Fort St. Michael at the mouth, Fort Gibbon near Tanana, Fort Rampart at Rampart, and Fort Egbert at Eagle. In addition, in May 1900 money was appropriated for construction of the Washington-Alaska Military Cable and Telegraph System (WAMCATS).

The army began construction of a telegraph line in 1900 after establishing a military post at Eagle in 1899. Initially, soldiers built a link from Eagle to the Canadian border so that messages could be dispatched over the Canadian line. At the same time survey work commenced for an all-American line following the Yukon River. By 1902 the line was in operation, and the army maintained and operated the communications until recent times. The officer in charge of construction of the line in the interior, Capt. Billy Mitchell, later became famous as an early advocate of air power.

Mile 1,431 (Valdez 275): Big Delta State Historical Park

The architectural and historic landmark of this seven-acre riverside park is Rika's Roadhouse, which was restored in 1986 and opened as a tourist attraction. The roadhouse was originally built by John Hajdukovich in 1910. He sold it to Rika Wallen, who had been roadhouse manager since 1917, in 1923. Rika became a well-known hostess on the highway and maintained the roadhouse until her retirement in the late 1940s. She continued to live in the roadhouse until her death in 1969.

John Hajdukovich was a pioneer trader who had a great impact on the Tanana region and on the Native Americans. Born in 1879 in Montenegro (now Yugoslavia), he emigrated to the United States in 1903 at age 23. In 1904 he moved to Juneau, Alaska, then joined the rush to Fairbanks by way of Whitehorse and Dawson City. For some years he trapped marten and other furbearing animals during the winter and prospected in the summer; he also hunted sheep, moose, and caribou for sale to the roadhouses on the Valdez-Fairbanks Trail.

As a trader among the Upper Tanana Indians from 1920, Hajdukovich became a strong advocate of their well-being. It was largely through his efforts that the Tetlin Indian Reserve was established in 1930. (See also Mile 1,301.7: Tetlin Junction.)

Mile 1,431.4: Big Delta Bridge

The Alyeska Pipeline crosses the Tanana on a bridge. This is the first sight of the famous pipeline available to travelers going north on the Alaska-Richardson highways.

The pipeline, carrying oil from the fields of Prudhoe Bay on the shores of the Arctic Ocean to Valdez for tanker shipment south, has been in operation since 1976. The Prudhoe Bay oil fields, the largest in North America, were discovered in 1968 by Atlantic Richfield and Exxon. Experts estimated that the fields held 9.6 billion barrels of oil and 26 trillion cubic feet of natural gas. Since the beginning of production the pipeline has carried approximately one-quarter of the United States production and 11 percent of the nation's consumption. At its peak the pipeline carried 1.5 million barrels per day to Valdez.

By 1986 it was determined that production had accounted for one-half of the reserve. Oil companies invested $2 billion in a waterflood project designed to maximize recovery by forcing additional oil from the reservoir rock and into producing wells.

The companies have recently completed the Central Gas facility, a plant capable of processing 3.7 billion cubic feet of natural gas amounting to more than 54,000 barrels of natural gas liquids daily. New fields have recently been opened for production, and oil exploration goes forward.

Extensive repairs were made on the pipeline in 1989–90 to remedy the effects of corrosion. There have not been any major spills causing environmental damage from the pipeline, although its construction in 1975 did have a serious impact on the environment through which it passed.

In 1987 the production of 716 million barrels of oil from Prudhoe Bay and Cook Inlet enabled Alaska to surpass Texas, the nation's longtime leader, in production.

Oil production has been a true bonanza for the state's economy. Oil income in taxes and royalties provides 85 percent of Alaska's general revenue. Since 1975 the state has collected $32 billion in revenues. On the dark side, Alaskans were shocked in April 1989 when a tanker heading out of Valdez crashed on Bligh Reef in Prince William Sound, losing most of its oil cargo. Containment efforts showed the oil companies had failed to prepare for such contingencies. Exxon spent millions of dollars on cleanup from 1989–91, but much of the damage to the environment and wildlife was irreparable.

Mile 1,444 (Valdez 288): View of the Alaska Range

To the south there is a view of three peaks of the Alaska Range: Mount Hayes (13,832 ft.), named for Charles Hayes of the U.S. Geological Survey; Hess Mountain (11,940 ft.), named for Mike Hess, a prospector of the 1890s; and Mount Deborah (12,339 ft.), named by Judge James Wickersham for his wife.

Mile 1,451 (Valdez 295): Site of Old Richardson Roadhouse

The roadhouse burned down in December 1982.

Mile 1,477.5 (Valdez 321.5): Harding Lake

Harding Lake was named for President Warren Harding, who visited Alaska in 1923 to dedicate the newly completed Alaska Railroad. Harding died shortly after his return outside. The Alaska Railroad, which is now operated by the state, runs from Seward to Fairbanks.

Mile 1,497 (Valdez 341): Eielson Air Force Base

The Eielson Air Force Base was a World War II construction project and remains an important military facility. It was named for pioneer bush pilot Carl Ben Eielson, who crashed in Siberia in 1929. In March 1991 the Soviet government conveyed the remains of Eielson's airplane to Fairbanks as a good-will gesture.

Mile 1,502.7 (Valdez 346.7): Chena Lake Recreation and Flood Control Area

Heavy rains in the summer of 1967 caused flooding of the Chena River and heavy damage to Fairbanks. To prevent other floods the U.S. Army Corps of Engineers constructed an earth dam, creating a lake that is a popular recreation spot.

Mile 1,505 (Valdez 349): Santa Claus House

Santa Claus House is a gift shop catering to visitors and mail order customers who are charmed to have dealings with North Pole despite its considerable distance from the geographic North Pole. The gift shop was established by Con Miller in 1949.

Mile 1,505.5 (Valdez 349.5): North Pole

North Pole is primarily a residential community for Fairbanks, the Eielson Airforce Base, and Fort Wainwright.

The area was originally homesteaded in 1944 by Bon V. Davis and named North Pole because he hoped to attract a toy manufacturer to the place.

Among leading industries is an oil refinery that produces fuel and other petroleum products from oil carried on the Alyeska Pipeline.

Mile 1,519 (Valdez 363): Fort Wainwright

Fort Wainwright is reached via Gaffney Road. This large army base was constructed during World War II and has been active ever since. It was named for Gen. Mayhew Wainwright, who was forced to surrender Bataan in the Philippine Islands to the Japanese forces in 1942.

Travelers whose destination is Fairbanks can go right on into the heart of the city to conclude an Alaska Highway–Richardson Highway journey of 1,520 miles.

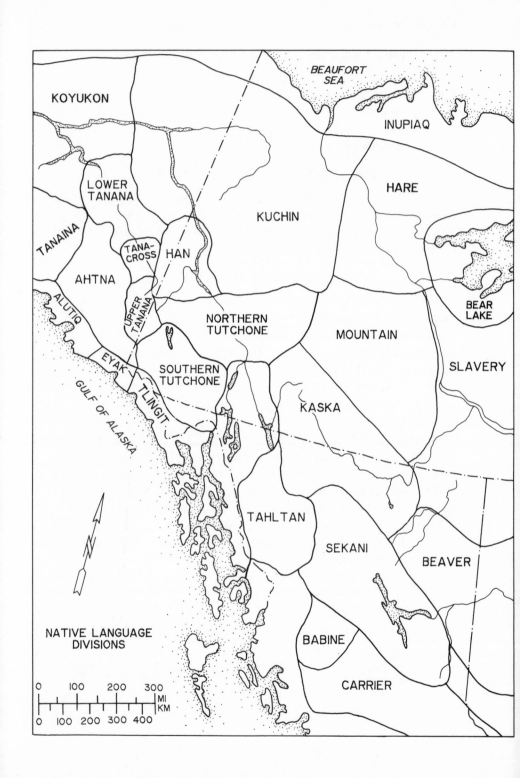

KOYUKON

BEAUFORT
SEA

INUPIAQ

HARE

LOWER
TANANA

KUCHIN

TANAINA

TANA-
CROSS

HAN

AHTNA

ALUTIQ

UPPER
TANANA

NORTHERN
TUTCHONE

BEAR
LAKE

MOUNTAIN

SLAVERY

EYAK

SOUTHERN
TUTCHONE

GULF OF ALASKA

TLINGIT

KASKA

TAHLTAN

SEKANI

BEAVER

NATIVE LANGUAGE
DIVISIONS

BABINE

0   100   200   300
                    MI
                    KM
0   100 200 300 400

CARRIER

Fairbanks:
The Golden Heart of Alaska

Took us a long time
Started slow
Now there's a road
Beginning to show.
— *The Big Road*

Alaskan Indians were not aggressive warriors like the mounted hunters of the western plains. Stampeders were welcomed rather than resisted. Miners were also of a different stamp from the gun-packing cowboys of other regions. The rigors of the North compelled people of both races to live as neighbors. And no Native Americans were forced from their traditional lands by the pressure of miners.

Generally, Natives posed neither a physical nor an economic threat to white settlement. Their contribution to the newcomers' development of their native land was substantial. As hunters they provided food; as trappers they gathered valuable furs for trade. They were good customers as well at the whites' stores.

The northern mining frontier offered natural hazards to the pioneer, but a kindly disposed aboriginal populace eased his lot. Native Americans saved the lives of innumerable prospectors who lost their way along the trails. No record exists of pioneers refusing the aid and hospitality of natives, who offered it regardless of their own poverty. Explorers on occasion owed their survival to such charity. In 1899, Lt. Joseph S. Herron led an expedition from Cook Inlet to explore the headwaters of the Kuskokwim River. In attempting to traverse a track-

159

less, swampy region, Herron lost his way; the horses became mired in the muck. Abandoning them, the panicked soldiers set out on foot for Fort Gibbon on the Yukon River. But for their discovery by the chief of the Tena Indians, the lost explorers would have died of starvation and exposure before finding their way out of the swamps. For two months the Indians sheltered the soldiers in their village before guiding them to the Tanana River, which they descended to Fort Gibbon.

During the same year, an army expedition to the Tanana River ran out of provisions. The soldiers ate their mules and stumbled on, clothing in shreds, shoeless, suffering from exposure and hunger. Just in time, they reached Tanana village, where they were received kindly. As Lt. Castner reported: "It is but justice to say a word for these friends of mine, who found us all but dead in the wilderness, with the Alaskan winter closing in around us. Entire strangers and of another race, they received us as no friend of mine, white or colored, ever did before or since. They asked no questions and required no credentials. They were men. It was enough that their fellow-beings were starving. Unknown to them were the wrongs our race have done theirs for centuries."

In time, roadhouses were established on trafficked trails, but amenities never developed on the scarcely used ones. Yet travelers could move lightly, without tent or stove, through any region populated by natives.

The only instance of violence by Indians against whites of the 1880s occurred in 1888, when prospector John Bremner was murdered. The response of miners was in sharp contrast to that of earlier decades. The slaying of trader James Beans's wife in 1878 had gone unpunished. Just four years earlier trader George Holt of the Alaska Commercial Company in Knik had been killed by Copper River Indians, but white men had not dared venture into the little-known Copper River country for revenge.

But with the death of Bremner, the pioneer prospector who had encountered Lt. Henry Allen's expedition in 1885, the Yukon whites determined that their security was at stake. Their numbers at Fortymile were great enough to ensure success, and the lower Koyukuk was not too far distant. As later reported by Henry Davis, the vigilantes voyaged to the Koyukuk, found the culprit, and hanged him: "Everybody pulled on the rope and tied him up and started for home. Everybody was satisfied and in good spirits."

Despite those few instances of hostility, however, white northerners generally acknowledged their debt to the Indians and adopted many of their ways. They learned to wear the Indian parka and mukluks and used native travel techniques. Native Americans were informal instructors in a school for survival, and whites who hoped to cope with the harsh climate were quick to learn. Despite this relationship, racial barriers did exist in Alaska. The stampeders' attitudes on race were fixed long before they journeyed north. In towns, if not on the trail, the whites felt themselves to be superior to the native people in all respects. It was not until recent times that Native Americans were permitted to serve on juries, although their right to hold mining claims was affirmed in early court decisions.

Natives of Alaska were free to live where they liked, and they were not scorned as were the immigrant Chinese and Japanese of the time. The despised Oriental, unlike the Native American, took jobs away from white men. Orientals were considered dangerous and were forcibly expelled from Juneau by a vigilante mob in 1886. Whites may have discriminated against Native Americans socially, but merchants welcomed their business.

Particular racial harmony existed outside of the towns. Men like George Pilcher, the woodcutter and trader of the lower Yukon, depended upon native society, entertaining his neighbors on long winter nights with gallons of tea and phonograph music. He and other similarly situated pioneers could hardly be intolerant: They traded with the men and bedded with the women.

Selling liquor to natives was a violation of law, and attempts to halt this illicit traffic greatly occupied law enforcement officials. It was an impossible task. The fulminations of the press against the sellers indicate the frustration involved: "The fear of God and the law should be put into the gizzards (they have no hearts) of the reptiles who furnish natives with fiery hootch," said one editor. Six months' imprisonment was the standard penalty imposed upon convicted liquor sellers, and prosecution for violation was vigorous. But comparatively few incidents resulted in prosecution. To many, the easy money to be gained in liquor transactions was too great a temptation. Then, too, so-called "squaw men," whites with Native American families, could buy booze freely and often acted as suppliers. Although many recognized the ravages of liquor, the white communities could do little to control its distribution.

Squaw men were sometimes scorned by other white folks, particularly women. Those who had married Native Americans suffered the bias of whites; those who forwent marriage altogether risked prosecution. The community and the court demanded that white men marry the women they lived with or leave them alone; the enforcement of the cohabitation law was vigorous.

Native people developed a taste for sugar and such luxury items as canned fruit and thereby committed themselves to a cash economy—a shift that was hardly suitable to the traditional pattern of subsistence. With a few exceptions, such as Creole John Minook, the discoverer of the Rampart gold field, Native Americans did not participate directly in prospecting and mining in the early days. They chopped wood, fished, and hunted for the miners in exchange for tobacco and other trading goods. At one time in the early mining period, most of the Yukon riverboats were piloted by natives.

Native Americans did find employment as miners after the early years as they became accustomed to the requirements of employment, and their labors were apparently accepted on the same terms as those of whites.

Natives Today. The Native Americans of Alaska and Canada have developed a strong sense of identity in recent decades. They have also gained in financial and political power because of land settlements made with their respective national governments. In Alaska in particular the native people have extended their economic reach through the corporations set up by the federal government as part of the land settlements.

Much tension exists among northern Native Americans. The issue of Native American sovereignty is a matter of lively controversy now before the courts. Assimilation is another issue: Some groups call for a preservation of traditional culture, whereas others emphasize the necessity of preparing the people to compete in the world at large. However such disputes are resolved, it is obvious that there will be great changes affecting all the residents of the North.

Mile 1,520: Fairbanks

The Tanana Valley was first explored by Lt. Henry Allen of the U.S. Army, who reached the great river by way of the upper Copper River in 1885. From the upper Copper River he crossed the Alaska Range to reach the Tanana River watershed. At the time the interior of Alaska through which the Tanana flowed was virtually unknown, but as increasing numbers of prospectors searched for gold in the interior they found their way into the Tanana Valley.

Trader E. T. Barnette, born in Ohio in 1863, had migrated to Montana in the 1880s, thence further west to Oregon, where in 1886 he was convicted of theft by bailee and served time in prison. In 1897 he joined the stampede to the Yukon, experienced some fleeting success as a profiteering merchant during Circle's post-Klondike prosperity, and earned the disdain of miners. Before setting up in Circle, he managed the mines of the North American Transportation and Trading Company at Dawson under John J. Healy's supervision.

Barnette remained in touch with Healy and acted on the older man's advice when he sought a new trading station. Go to Tanacross, urged Healy. Tanacross, or Tanana Crossing (Mile 1,325.8 on the Alaska Highway), was the point on the Tanana River where the Valdez-Eagle Trail reached the river. In 1900 there was not much doing in the area, but Healy was planning a railroad, and a Tanacross station would be important. The railroad would end the remoteness of the Tanana region and spur gold prospecting and probable discovery of rich fields.

Barnette followed Healy's advice, announcing to Dawson newsmen his plan to found another Chicago serving 50,000 square miles of the Tanana Valley, a region of fine agricultural and mineral prospects. In San Francisco he found a backer, bought $20,000 in trade goods, and in 1901 pushed up the Yukon and Tanana. The steamer *Lavelle Young* could not reach Tanana because of low water, so Barnette turned up the Chena, a small tributary.

Gold Strikes. It was Barnette's good fortune that Felix Pedro and Tom Gilmore showed up to patronize his store in 1901. Pedro, a veteran prospector who had outfitted in Circle for his trek into the Tanana country, gladdened Barnette's heart by revealing his discovery of promising gold signs. Chena boomed as the news spread of Pedro's discovery. Several other towns rose in the region, including Fairbanks.

Felix Pedro was no tyro in northern prospecting. He had worked at Caribou, British Columbia, in 1893, at Fortymile, and in the Klondike before prospecting on the Tanana. Barnette sent word of the strike to Dawson City, hoping to attract a crowd of customers. Dawson men rushed to the Tanana but were disappointed when they did not find rich claims at once. Most mushed back to Dawson City. Those who remained and other prospectors who came in 1903–04 did find gold, and the camp's prosperity was assured.

It was in March 1903 that Judge James Wickersham heard about the rich strikes in the Tanana Valley. Wickersham had held the first court in the interior at Eagle, Circle, and Rampart in 1900 and knew that the interior needed a major gold strike if large communities were ever to develop. He was pleased that the center of activity was Fairbanks because he had named the place before seeing it. While Barnette was making preparations at St. Michael for his founding voyage Wickersham had suggested the name of the senator from Indiana, Charles Warren Fairbanks, for the location of Barnette's trading post.

Wickersham and the Tanana Valley. In hearing the news of the gold strike, Wickersham considered ordering soldiers from Fort Gibbon to Fairbanks but decided to have a look at the camp himself before doing so. In April he set out from Circle with a six-dog team and a driver. The route he traveled was fairly well populated, and he found a cabin to stay at each night. One stormy night he found himself one of eight people crowded into a cabin measuring twelve by twelve feet. It was as dirty as it was stuffy, but the lady of the house provided good sourdough pancakes for breakfast, and that compensated.

Wickersham fell in love with the Tanana Valley at first sight; its vastness and verdant grandeur moved him as no other scene in the North. Standing on the brow of a hill overlooking the valley, he took in its expanse and found it unrivaled in natural beauty. Scattered about the valley were abundant stretches of evergreen forests and the "rising waters of the Tanana, in lake-like spaces, sparkling in the midday sun." In the distant east and west "as far as the eye can reach, and to the base of the snowy range along its southern bounds, the unfretted valley is carpeted with evergreen."

Beyond the Tanana River (which he liked to call the Ohio-of-the-North) stood the colossal Alaska Range, capped by many peaks: "To the eastward they descend, one behind another until the distant horizon limits the vision but not the range." He recognized Mount Hayes, Mount Deborah, Hess Mountain, and to the west, Mount McKinley. "This mountain is to the Tena, what it must always remain to all tribes of men in this region, Denali, the high one."

The Tanana is the greatest and longest tributary of the Yukon. Rising near the Canadian border, it winds its way northwest for hundreds of miles before joining the Yukon. The few Indians dwelling along its banks called the imposing waterway the Tanana, "river of the mountain," and found it rich in life-giving salmon, not knowing or caring about its history or hidden treasures. For hundreds of miles the river churns its way through a valley of surpassing beauty.

But the Tanana does have a history, an ancient one that explains why, among all the rivers of the interior, its tributaries became so rich in gold. To the geologist, the presence of gold is no mystery. Placer deposits, streaks of gold, are found at bedrock in the gravel of old streambeds. Perhaps as long as 150 million years ago the bedrock surface of the valley was pierced by hot, molten rocks forced up from below by some raging turmoil in the bowels of the earth. This intrusion lifted and cracked the bedrock in many places, leaving small veins into which the fiery mixture of rock and mineral flowed. Ages passed, and the fissured bedrock was uplifted and eroded. The lighter rocks and minerals were broken down and removed by the streams, but the gold accumulated in the creek bottoms, to be covered by later erosion products. A permanently frozen crust as deep as 70 feet, and often more, obscured and protected the precious metal that lay beneath. The gold was there, though hard to reach, and men would have it despite all.

The Garden of Alaska. Wickersham continued his travels into the new gold region. On reaching Pedro Creek, site of the first strikes, the judge talked with a successful Italian prospector, Jack Costa. He described Costa's "happy, smiling face like the full moon over the Ketchumstock hills—[as he] emerges from his pit, he remarked—probably for the thousandth time—'By Godde, I gotte de gold.'"

After a meal at Jujuira Wada's restaurant the judge appointed J. Tod Cowles justice of peace and accepted Frank Cleary's offer of a corner lot for the jail. A representative of Chena called on the Judge to petition him to locate the court there rather than in Fairbanks. Chena seemed a more logical center than Fairbanks for the principal town of the region. It was located at the head of steamer navigation on the Tanana, whereas Fairbanks was up the Chena slough a few miles. Fairbanks's big advantage, apart from Barnette's store, was its greater proximity to the creeks where the mining was being done. This proximity and the fact that Judge Wickersham had named the town caused him to assign the court to Fairbanks. The choice thwarted the development of Chena, which faded away after a few years. Today virtually nothing remains of the Chena town site, which has long since been washed away by the Tanana River.

The day following the judge's arrival was cold and clear. Though the temperature the night before had fallen to twenty degrees below zero, the afternoon was bathed in warm sunshine. It was spring, and spring promotes optimism. The judge felt that the Tanana Valley would one day be the garden of Alaska, where as many as one million people might reside. Wickersham observed unfolding pussy willows and cattails and gathered a bouquet of birch limbs with swollen buds. Overhead appeared other harbingers of spring, great flocks of geese heading for their summer nesting in the Yukon flats. These lovely fowl always rested for a time in the Tanana Valley before winging onward. Before long the judge observed the most significant sign of spring, when with a roar the rivers opened. The Tanana opened first, then the Chena; soon the streams of the entire valley were flooding down toward the parent river, the Yukon.

Wickersham's account of these exciting events in his memoir, *Old Yukon*, is a fine piece of writing. Since the judge kept a diary during his Alaskan years, it is interesting to look at his comments over those early days in the Tanana Valley. Even the script of his diary shows his excitement. In recording his sensations on a beautiful morning that first May in Fairbanks, Wickersham betrayed joy and ebullience in his oversize, looping, exuberant penmanship as he anticipated warmer weather. Nature abounded. "Ducks, geese, robins, birds, squirrels — the woods are vocal with animal and bird song." Again he rhapsodized, "the Tanana Valley is the garden spot of Alaska."

The judge had high hopes for the people of the Fairbanks camp. The crowd was a motley one, "sourdoughs and cheechacos [tenderfeet], miners, gamblers, Indians, Negroes, Japanese, prostitutes, music, drinking! It's rough but healthy — the beginning — I hope, of an American Dawson."

The first banquet in the Tanana Valley took place at the Tokyo Restaurant. What bore this grand name was just another one-room log cabin. Judge Wickersham invited all the members of the bar and the camp's leading citizens. (Lawyers always had much work in mining camps, what with claim jumping and the general confusion resulting from imprecise locating of claims. Seven members of the bar were already on hand by the spring of 1903, and more were on their way.)

Drinks were served from the old gold pan with which Felix Pedro had made his original discovery. The pan was presented to Wickersham, who promised to send it on to Senator Fairbanks along with a bottle of gold dust.

The first newspaper published in the valley was written entirely by the judge. Entitled the *Fairbanks Miner*, it was filled with local news and ads and sold for $5 a copy. Only one issue appeared; its primary reason for being was to provide Wickersham and a party the money they would need to outfit themselves for a Mount McKinley climbing excursion. Three copies were given away to be read in the saloons; one went outside to Senator Fairbanks.

Publication day turned out to be breakup day on the Chena River as well. Wickersham marveled at this "wonderful manifestation of the natural force of water and ice. It came down suddenly without warning and in five minutes the ice was pushing into the woods breaking into great sections, grinding, rolling and tearing, an irresistible flood of ice, mud and water." Then soon, all flags flying and whistle shrilling, came the first steamboat of the season, loaded with friends, relatives, and fresh provisions.

Among his concerns for native culture, the judge had strong feelings about the preservation of native placenames. He mocked Lt. Henry Allen, the Copper River explorer, for naming Mount Sanford for his grandfather, echoing the protest of natives. Yaho, the grandfather of the Tena people, had named the mountain for Kuhltan. "But what's a heathen god or two, or a string of Indians in legends, particularly those of a helpless tribe of savages," said arrogant whites, compared with the vanity of white ancestry? "The Tena legends and gods were ruthlessly brushed aside by the official report, prepared in musty offices in Washington, and approved and printed by the government of the United States. Kuhltan, the glorious Alaska mountain, revered by the Atna people, became a stranger's great-grandfather's monument." What happened to Kuhltan, Wickersham said, also occurred to many other Alaska mountains, rivers, and commanding natural objects, which "were shamelessly misnamed by vain officials, with the approval of government departments in the capital of a civilized nation."

Fairbanks developed as Wickersham hoped and became the largest town in Alaska. The entire Tanana prospered after the Fairbanks gold field proved to be long lasting. By 1904, Fairbanks boasted 387 log houses and 1,000 residents, with another 1,000 living along various creeks in the region.

It was always a special place to its residents. Its cold winters suited some folks, but others liked to winter outside if they could afford it. Each fall the last river steamboats took out a goodly portion of the population, and in the spring the same boats brought them back.

Ben Dowling's Dogs. Dog teams were generally relied on before they were replaced by autos and airplanes. Stalwart dog mushers such as Ben Downing carried the mail in the early days. Downing had not known much about dogs before coming to Alaska because he had been a mule driver in Missouri, but he soon learned. He did not have anything to learn about trading, however, judging from the episode of the dispirited dog.

Ben had sold an ailing dog to a less experienced man. Some months passed, and the new owner began to feel that he had been imposed upon. The dog Downing sold him was not earning its keep, being too sickly to do its proper share of sled hauling. The buyer called on Downing and complained.

"Good dog," responded Ben enthusiastically. "Fine dog. Always did think a whole lot of that dog. I love my dogs."

"But he is sick," repeated the buyer. "Was sick when I bought him."

Ben was surprised: "I fed him good. I always do feed my dogs good."

"But he is sick," screamed the buyer.

"Sick?" says Ben. "Oh, homesick. I always did treat my dogs well and feed them good."

The Tanana Valley's Importance

The Tanana Valley development was arguably the most significant one in Alaska's early history. While the Seward Peninsula was somewhat richer, the Tanana yield was sustained for decades, and the location assured permanent communities in the vast heartland drained by the Yukon River. Tanana's wealth also guaranteed the long-term existence of a trail-road network commencing from the coast at Valdez. Originally, the government trail from Valdez ran to Eagle on the Yukon, but the Fairbanks stampede resulted in a diversion to the Tanana. Over the 376-mile route, winter and summer trails were maintained and served by the stage coaches of the Ed S. Orr Stage Company. Passengers paid $150 to ride to Fairbanks, and a modest amount of freight was carried at fifty to seventy-five cents per pound. Depending upon the season, horse or dog relay teams were placed at roadhouses along the way so the journey could be made in nine days.

Yukon River transport remained important in serving Fairbanks. Passengers could reach the new town in season from St. Michael or the upper Yukon, and the boats could handle large freight that was beyond the capacity of stagecoaches.

Technological Progress. The early placer mining methods gave way for the most part to more advanced technology after the Klondike discovery. Drift mining underground was an expedient that took advantage of permafrost. Miners could dig underground from their entry shaft without shoring the tunnels tunnels extensively with timber and without the need to pump away excess water. Yet drift mining was basically a pick-and-shovel method of production, slow and cumbersome and only capable of mining bedrock, thus wasting any gold in the overburden.

Advancing from drift mining to more effective mining techniques required expensive machinery and more capital. The independent miner of the pre-Klondike period almost became an anachronism as time passed, yet the transition was inevitable under the circumstances. Costs of mining in Alaska were always higher than elsewhere because of freight charges and peculiar ground conditions.

Established western mining methods included open-cut, hydraulic, and dredging. All of these were used singly or in combination in Alaska depending upon conditions, but there were some adaptations of each method in the North. Each method had its disadvantages. Open-cut mining—digging long, narrow trenches—required the use of steam scrapers and other heavy expensive equipment, so it was not commonly practiced. Hydraulic mining, used in combination with open-cut and dredging operations, was usually a muck-stripping operation. Since hydraulic operations required lots of water, a scarce item in most mining districts, its operation necessitated the construction of reservoirs, ditches, and flumes. Dredging, of course, required the bulkiest and most expensive item of equipment available. And, to aggravate the high costs of mining by any method, the factor of operating time had to be weighed. In most mining districts, the season ran from June to September, thus sharply reducing the profit-making time and lengthening the exposure of equipment to fire, flood, and other destructive forces.

From 1908–15 it became increasingly obvious that the richest ground of areas like the Tanana had yielded all it held to hand, sluicing, and drifting methods. Tests showed that the worked tailings and ground could still be mined profitably by the most advanced mining technology. Advanced technology meant dredges. These expensive machines became increasingly common from 1916, and production justified the heavy expense involved. A U.S. Geological Survey report of 1936 noted that nearly 79 percent of all the placer gold produced in Alaska that year was mined by dredges.

The Fairbanks Exploration Company. The revival of interior mining with the introduction of dredges in 1916 was sustained by the entry of the Fairbanks Exploration Co. (F.E. Co.), a subsidiary of the United States Refining and Mining Company. In 1923 the company acquired the Hammon Consolidated Gold Fields, the major dredging operation of the Nome region. The next year the company started investigating the Fairbanks region and acquiring properties. Large-scale dredging operations carried on until 1938. A major project supporting mining involved the construction of the Davidson Ditch, carrying water for mining from the Chatanika River to workings on Cleary, Goldstream, and other creeks for a distance of ninety miles.

Prospecting was done with churn drills using standard six-inch tools and thin placer bits. Test results varied greatly because some holes penetrated old drift mine workings while others were sunk in ground untouched by earlier miners. But since it had been determined early that even previously mined ground could be dredged profitably, the company could make a reasonable assessment of the values of different properties. In acquiring those properties the F.E. Co. benefited from the general doldrums in mining activity at the time. Most miners realized that long-term production from their claims could be achieved only through dredging and were receptive to sale or lease offers. The lease option offered by the company was a strong inducement to miners who believed strongly that their claims were rich and wished to retain a share of expected earnings.

The eight dredges operating in the Fairbanks area did a good deal of work and moved much earth. In the first stage of the operation the ground had to be stripped and thawed, then flooded for the dredge's passage. After dredges finished their work on Goldstream, Cleary, Pedro, Fish, and Cripple creeks in the 1920s and 1930s some were moved, at great difficulty, in the 1940s and 1950s to new ground on Fairbanks, Chicken, Eldorado, Dome, and Ester creeks.

Modern Fairbanks

The dredge mining of the Tanana kept Fairbanks prosperous for a number of years. Mining was prohibited during World War II, but wartime construction and the big military bases of Fort Wainwright and Eielson provided plenty of employment. Gold mining did not revive after the war as had been hoped, but Fairbanks held the growing campus of the University of Alaska and was the service center for the Arctic and a large part of the interior. Anchorage grew even faster during the war and after and surpassed Fairbanks as the territory's largest city.

Fairbanks and Alaska have always known economic booms and busts, but the defense spending for the Distant Early Warning Line and other military projects kept Fairbanks busy during the 1950s and 1960s. In the mid-1970s the construction of the Alyeska Pipeline put Fairbanks at the center of activity, and the old mining town did well until the statewide recession of the 1980s, from which it has lately rebounded.

The economy of Fairbanks and other parts of Alaska has always affected the traffic on the Alaska Highway. When times are good in the North, there are likely to be more cars, vans, trucks, and campers heading up the highway loaded with hopeful families keen to respond to one of the state's slogans: "North to the Future."

Last Words

Midway in the postconstruction history of the road, the late 1960s, a traveler made the round trip with the intent of writing a traveler's companion. Edward McCourt confessed he did not know the highway well but figured that his impressions were of some value. His book, *Yukon and Northwest Territories*, is interesting, but his concluding statement must be refuted. "It is a road without people and without history," he wrote. "Built in 1942 to meet the menace of invasion from Japan, it served its original purpose for a year or two . . . but no armies marched north or south on the Highway, no blood except that drawn by black flies has so far stained its surface."

George R. Stewart, who traveled the route in 1957, also believed the highway lacked historical association, and he urged the government to place more markers. Stewart found it hard to find information about the area before construction of the highway for his book *N.A.I.: Looking North*.

What confused McCourt in part about the lack of history and sustained purpose of the road was his Canadian orientation. He did not travel or look beyond Whitehorse before returning to dash up the Mackenzie Highway, and he failed to recognize the highway's usefulness to Alaskans. Thus he wrote: "The road is not like any other road. Other roads are built through populated areas; they link small towns and great cities; they bear a substantial human traffic and enormous burdens of freight."

But in 1968 it was McCourt's view that "the Alaska Highway is a ribbon of gravel—and occasional hardtop—running inside Canadian territory for 1,200 miles and Alaskan territory for two hundred more. It has a beginning and an end and almost nothing in between." Maybe McCourt saw the tortuous road with the eye of a disgruntled taxpayer, one wondering why an expensive road wandered through a country where the population density was one person to every twenty square miles: "In proportion to its length and the cost of upkeep, the number of persons and the quantity of goods it carries are infinitesimal."

Yet even McCourt was not impervious to the romance of the road. As he wheeled out of Dawson Creek he felt the unique attraction of this "very different road, the only road on the continent that points to the High North. It stirs unfamiliar emotions, excites strange dreams, for in itself it is not like any road we have so far known, and it leads to far off places of earth that few of us have ever seen."

Since McCourt's time many more people have traveled "the Big Road." What might happen in the next fifty years on the highway cannot be known, but passage to the North on the Alaska Highway is not likely to lose its interest and excitement.

Suggested Reading

Berton, Pierre. *Klondike: The Last Great Gold Rush*. Toronto: McClelland & Stewart, 1972.

Coates, Ken S., and William R. Morrison. *Land of the Midnight Sun: A History of the Yukon*. Edmonton: Hurtig, 1988.

Cole, Terrence. *E.T. Barnette: The Strange Story of the Man Who Founded Fairbanks*. Edmonds: Alaska Northwest, 1981.

Coutts, R. *Yukon Places and Names*. Sidney, B.C.: Gray's Publishing, 1980.

Hunt, William R. *Distant Justice: Policing the Alaska Frontier*. Norman, OK: University of Oklahoma, 1987.

———. *North of 53: The Wild Days of the Alaska Yukon Mining Frontier 1870–1914*. New York: Macmillan, 1974.

McCandless, Robert G. *Yukon Wildlife: A Social History*. Edmonton: University of Alberta, 1985.

McClellan, Catherine. *Part of the Land, Part of the Water: A History of the Yukon Indians*. Vancouver: Douglas and McIntyre, 1987.

McCourt, Edward. *Yukon and Northwest Territories*. Toronto: Macmillan, 1969.

MacGregor, J.G. *Klondike Rush Through Edmonton*. Toronto: McClelland and Stewart, 1970.

Milepost, The, 3rd ed. Anchorage: Alaska Research Co., 1952.

Milepost, The, 43rd ed. Bothell, WA: Alaska Northwest, 1991.

Naske, Claus. *Paving Alaska's Trails: The Work of the Alaska Road Commission*. New York: University Press of America, 1986.

Naske, Claus-M., and Herman Slotnick. *State of Alaska: A History of the 49th State*. Norman, OK: University of Oklahoma, 1987.

Phillips, James W. *Alaska-Yukon Place Names*. Seattle: University of Washington, 1973.

Remley, David. *The Crooked Road: The Story of the Alaska Highway*. New York: McGraw-Hill, 1976.

Rosten, Norman. *The Big Road*. New York: Macmillan, 1946.

Stewart, George. *N.A.I.: Looking North*. Boston: Houghton Mifflin, 1957.

Webb, Melody. *The Last Frontier: A History of the Yukon Basin of Canada and Alaska*. Albuquerque: University of New Mexico, 1985.

Wickersham, James. *Old Yukon: Old Tales, Trails, and Trials*. St. Paul: West Publishing, 1938.

Woolcock, Iris. *The Road North: One Woman's Adventure Driving the Alaska Highway 1947–1948*. ed. Edward Bovy. Anchorage: Greatland Graphics, 1990.

Young, Gerri F. *The Fort Nelson Story*. Fort Nelson: Gerri Young, 1980.

Index